MIDLANDS FOOTBALL GROUNDS
FROM THE AIR

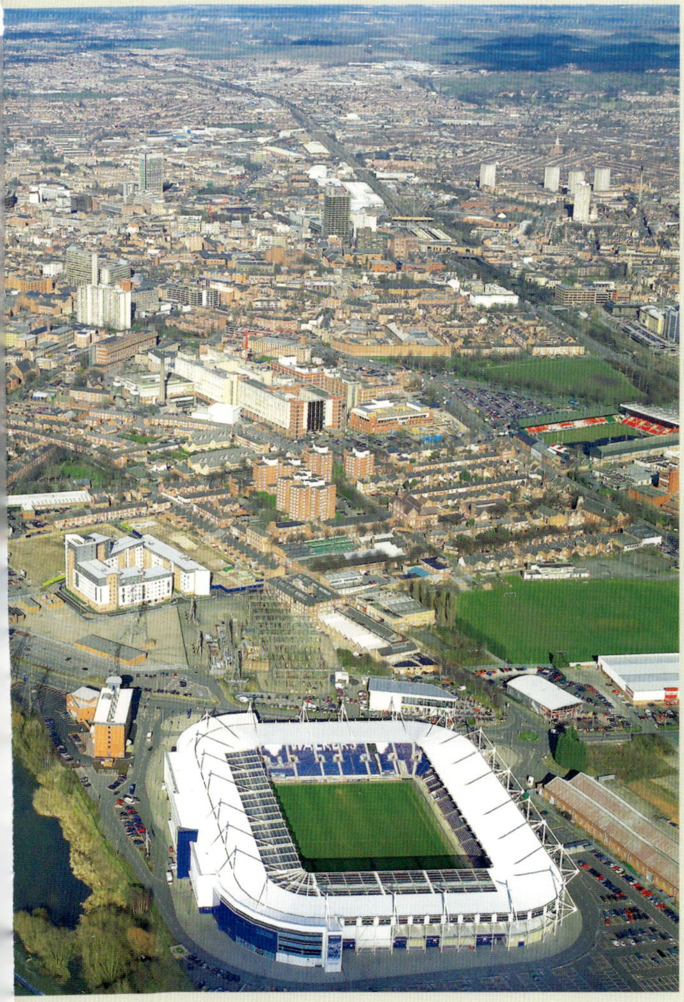

MYRIAD
LONDON

ASTON VILLA

Aston Villa was formed by members of the Villa Cross Wesleyan Chapel in 1874. The club moved to the Aston Lower grounds in 1896 after spending 20 years at a basic ground on Wellington Road. The site was a leisure park dating back to the 1870s but had fallen into a state of disrepair. Villa began developing the ground, building a main stand on what had been a sub-tropical garden. Banking was raised on the other three sides of the ground and a basic barrel roof was added to the Trinity Road side. The ground opened in 1897, the same year Villa won the League and Cup double. Attendances continued to rise and prior to the First World War Villa were drawing in regular crowds of 26,000. In 1914 Villa realised their plans for future development of the ground. The work began with the removal of the concrete cycle path, which had run around the pitch; both end terraces were banked and another terrace added to the front of the Witton Lane Stand. After the war the Trinity Road Stand was built, a stand which was so extravagant in design it cost the club £89,810. The Holte End was extended during the Second World War and in 1946 Villa Park saw its highest ever crowd of 76,588. Villa Park's selection as a location for World Cup games brought about further developments with seats being added to the ground's terracing. The two-tiered North Stand was built in 1977, with further developments coming in the light of the Taylor report.

In 1990 the Holte End terracing was updated and the roof extended but as a result of poor planning the whole structure had to be demolished in 1994 and replaced with a two-tier stand. Trinity Road Stand was refurbished in time for the 1996 European Championships. In order to maintain a capacity in excess of 40,000 the club set about planning to redevelop the Witton Lane Stand (now the Doug Ellis Stand). There are now plans to redevelop and enlarge the North Stand.

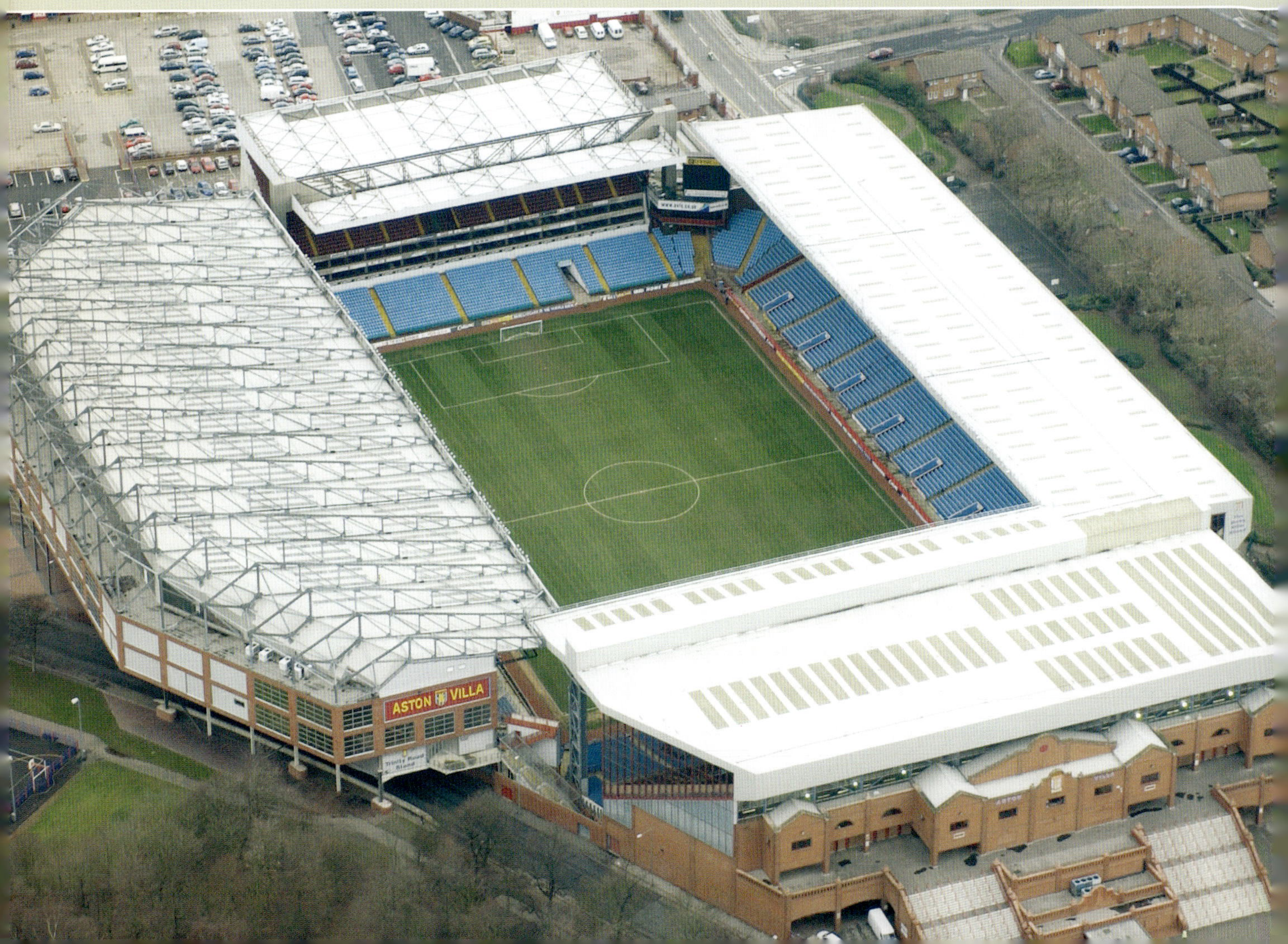

Ground: **Villa Park**
Address: Villa Park, Birmingham B6 6HE
Capacity: 42,551
Pitch dimensions: 105m x 69m (115 x 72 yards)
Record attendance: 76,588 vs Derby County, March 2 1946

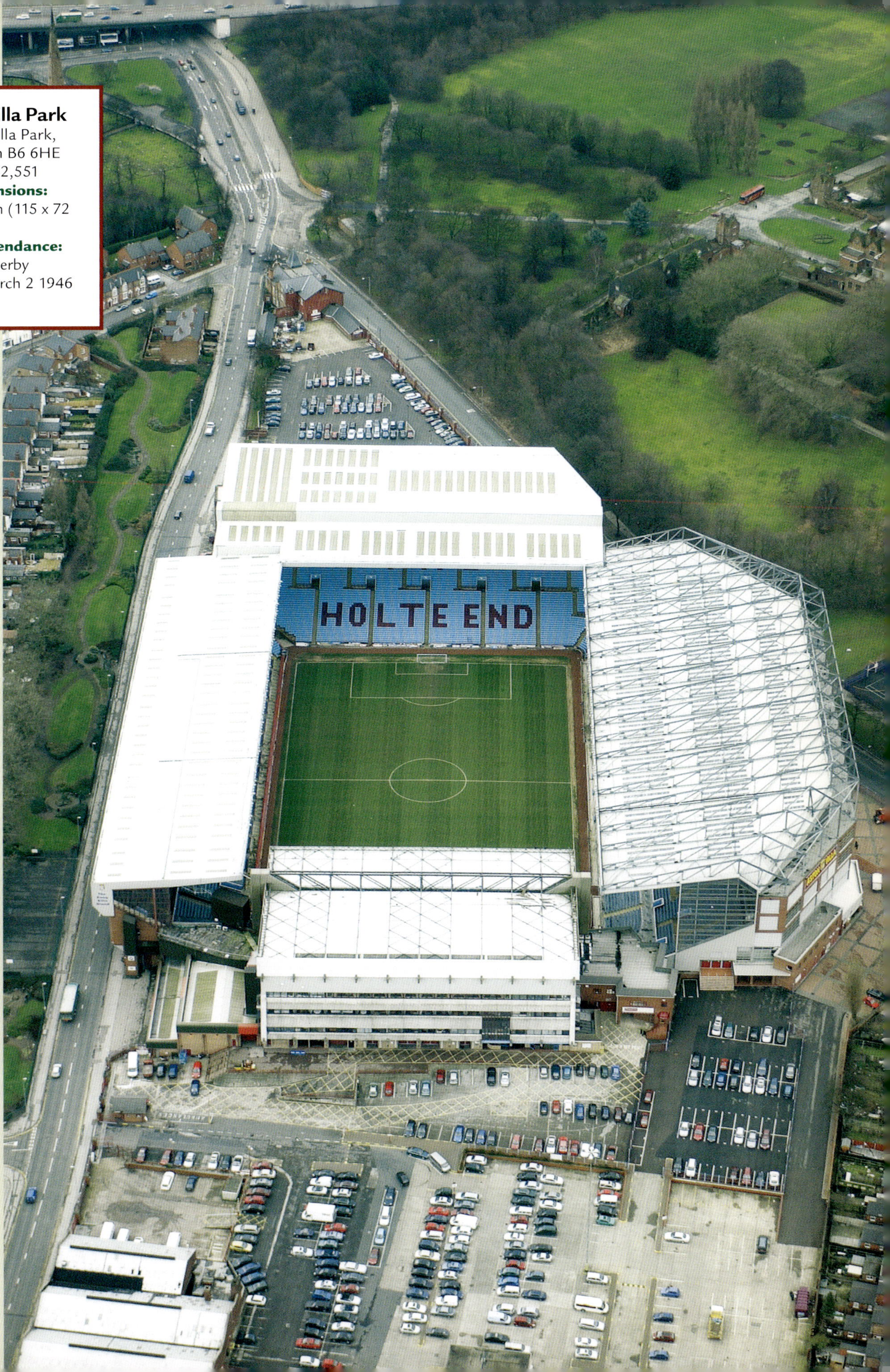

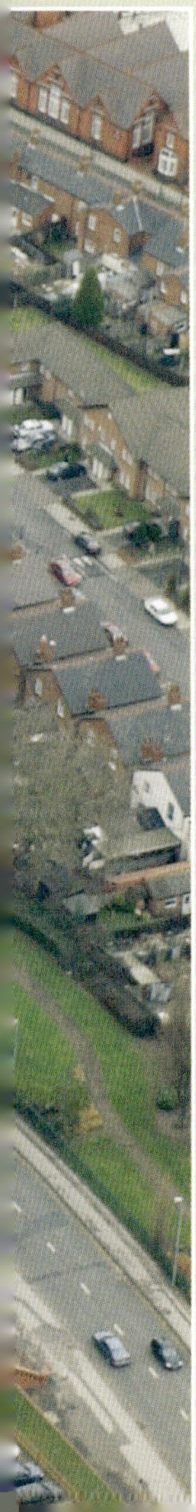

BIRMINGHAM CITY

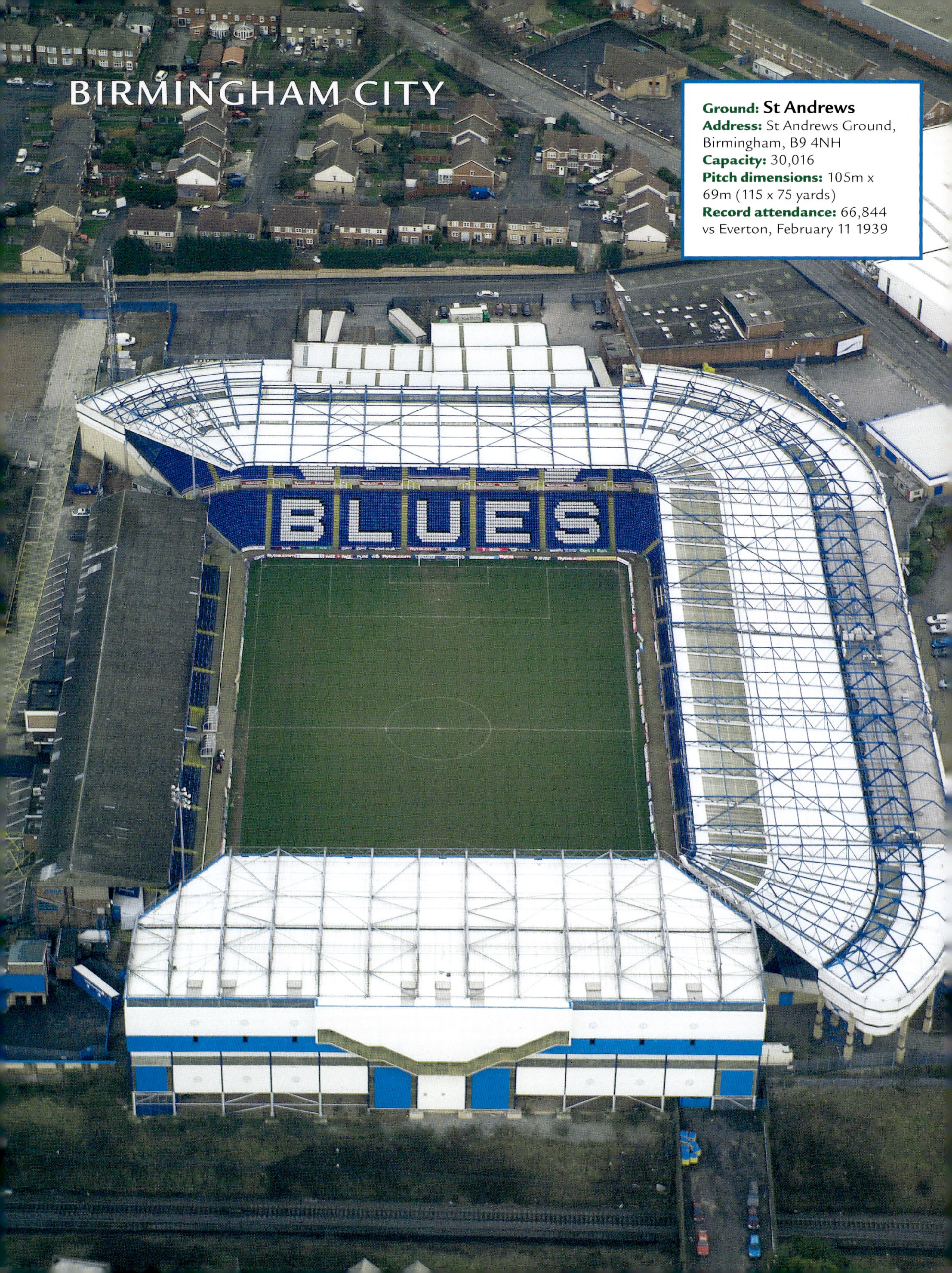

Ground: St Andrews
Address: St Andrews Ground, Birmingham, B9 4NH
Capacity: 30,016
Pitch dimensions: 105m x 69m (115 x 75 yards)
Record attendance: 66,844 vs Everton, February 11 1939

Birmingham City FC started as the Small Heath Alliance in 1875. Their first pitch was on waste ground on Arthur Street but as their crowd of followers grew, they moved to Muntz Street, where they remained for the next 29 years. The club turned professional in 1885 and changed their name to Birmingham FC in 1905. The Blues moved to St Andrews in 1906, onto a ground that had been previously occupied by gypsies, who are said to have laid a curse on it. The massive Main Stand was built and in order to raise the height of the ground beneath terracing on the Coventry Road End, locals were encouraged to dump rubbish on the site. A Kop terrace was built on top of the accumulated spoil, with a capacity of 48,000. Terrace covers had been put on top of the Railway End and the Kop by the time the ground recorded its highest gate ever of 66,844 in 1939. During the Second World War the curse returned: the ground was damaged by bombs over 20 times and the Main Stand burned down when a fireman inadvertently used petrol instead of water to put out a brazier. Birmingham had to move, first to Leamington and then to Villa Park until 1943, while their ground was repaired. They emerged from the war with a new name, Birmingham City FC. The Kop reopened in 1947 and the new two-tiered Main Stand opened in 1954. Success in Europe funded the building of the Railway End Stand in 1963-4.

The 1980s saw a run of bad luck, and by 1989 the Blues found themselves in the Third Division. But March 1993 saw the Blues' fortunes improve as David Sullivan took over ownership of the club. Sullivan drew up plans for a £4.5m development of the Kop and Tilton Road End, which opened in 1994; in 1999 the Railway End was redeveloped and there are now plans to develop the Main Stand sometime in the future.

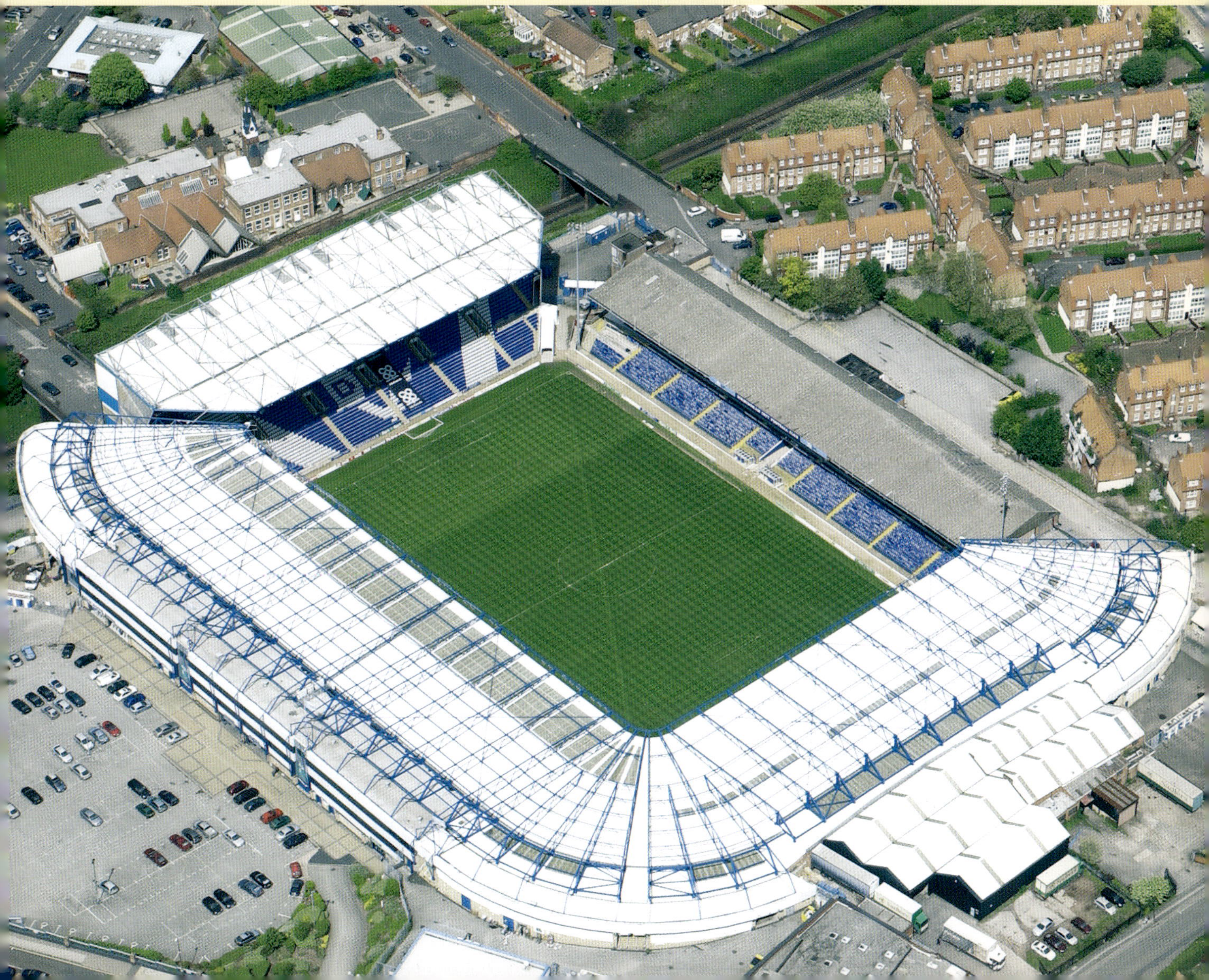

CHESTERFIELD

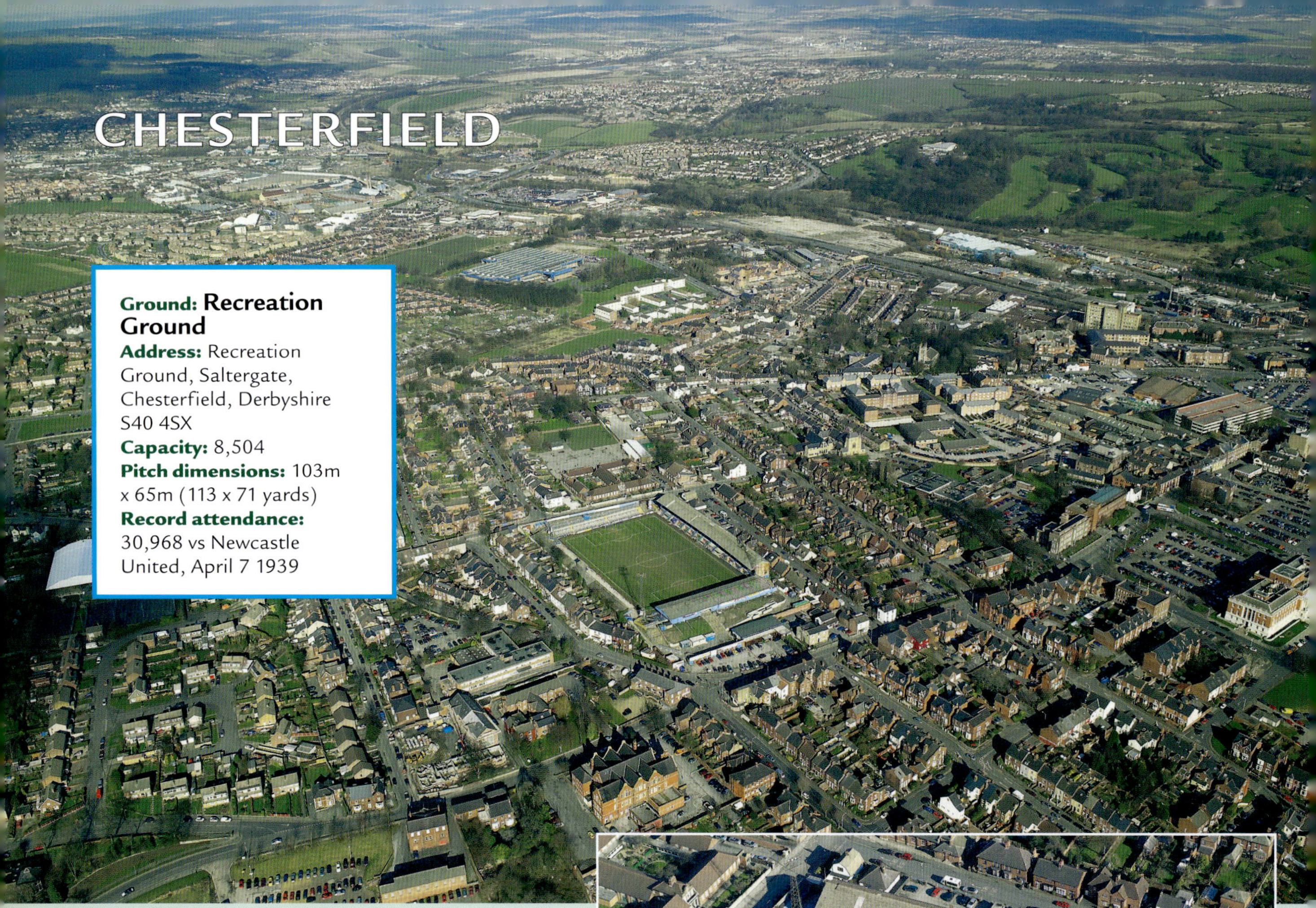

Ground: **Recreation Ground**
Address: Recreation Ground, Saltergate, Chesterfield, Derbyshire S40 4SX
Capacity: 8,504
Pitch dimensions: 103m x 65m (113 x 71 yards)
Record attendance: 30,968 vs Newcastle United, April 7 1939

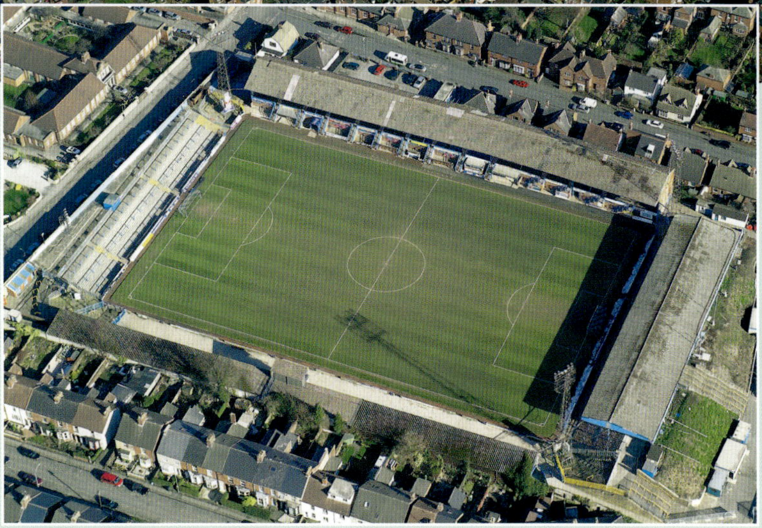

Chesterfield can trace its roots back to 1866 and a team originally called Chesterfield Town. The club settled at the Recreation Ground in 1887 after playing at various local grounds. At the turn of the century a small stand stood along the east side of the pitch, and a pavilion was built in 1914. After a 10-year spell in the League between 1899 and 1909, Chesterfield FC rejoined the League in 1921, but it was not until the 1930s that they began developing the ground. The Main Stand was opened in 1936, and just three years later a record attendance of 30,968 watched the Spireites take on Newcastle United in a Second Division match. A successful Cup run in the 1950s funded a cover over the Compton Street Terrace, and in 1961 a cover was added to the Kop. The Spireites were the last League club to instal floodlights. After several failed attempts, the Recreation Ground finally erected floodlights in 1967. The various acts aiming to improve safety at football grounds, which came into force in the 1980s and 1990s, saw capacity at the Recreation Ground drop from 19,750 to 8,504. Chesterfield, like many other clubs, found the financial commitments needed to meet the new regulations extremely demanding. Its location, with surrounding housing, means further development of some of the stands and terraces would be difficult if not impossible. The Compton Street Terrace was replaced by an all-seater stand in 2002; however it appears the death knell has now sounded for the Recreation Ground. The club has announced plans to move to a 10,000 capacity stadium on the site of a former glass factory.

Crewe Alexandra formed in 1877, although their roots go back to an athletics club founded in 1866. The club's name "Alexandra" is thought to have been in honour of Princess Alexandra, who married Prince Edward in 1863. Early games were played at Nantwich Road, where a recreation ground had the capacity to stage cricket, football and cycling. Crewe reached the semi-finals of the FA Cup in 1888, an achievement they have never since matched or beaten. They moved grounds twice in 1896, before returning to the recreation ground. In 1906 the building of new railway lines forced the club to move again, this time to Gresty Road. The ground had a stand on each side of the pitch and some embankments. It was 1921 when Crewe joined the League for a second time after a short spell from 1892-1896. The original Main Stand burned down in 1932 and a new one was built in its place, on the south side of the pitch.

A record 20,000 supporters saw Crewe take on Spurs in the FA Cup in 1960, but little development took place over the course of the next 30 years, except for the rebuilding of the Popular Side in the 1970s. Gresty Road was transformed during the 1990s however. Seats were added to all of the existing stands, and the Gresty Road End had a cantilevered roof added in 1995 along with 994 seats. The Popular Side had seats added and the roof is now supported with just two poles instead of 12 columns. A large, single-tiered cantilevered stand, the Air Products Stand, was built in 1999 to replace the Railtrack Stand. It now dominates one whole side of the ground, and has a capacity of 7,000. There are plans to develop the Blue Bell BMW Stand (formerly the Popular Side) and turn it into a two-tiered stand.

CREWE ALEXANDRA

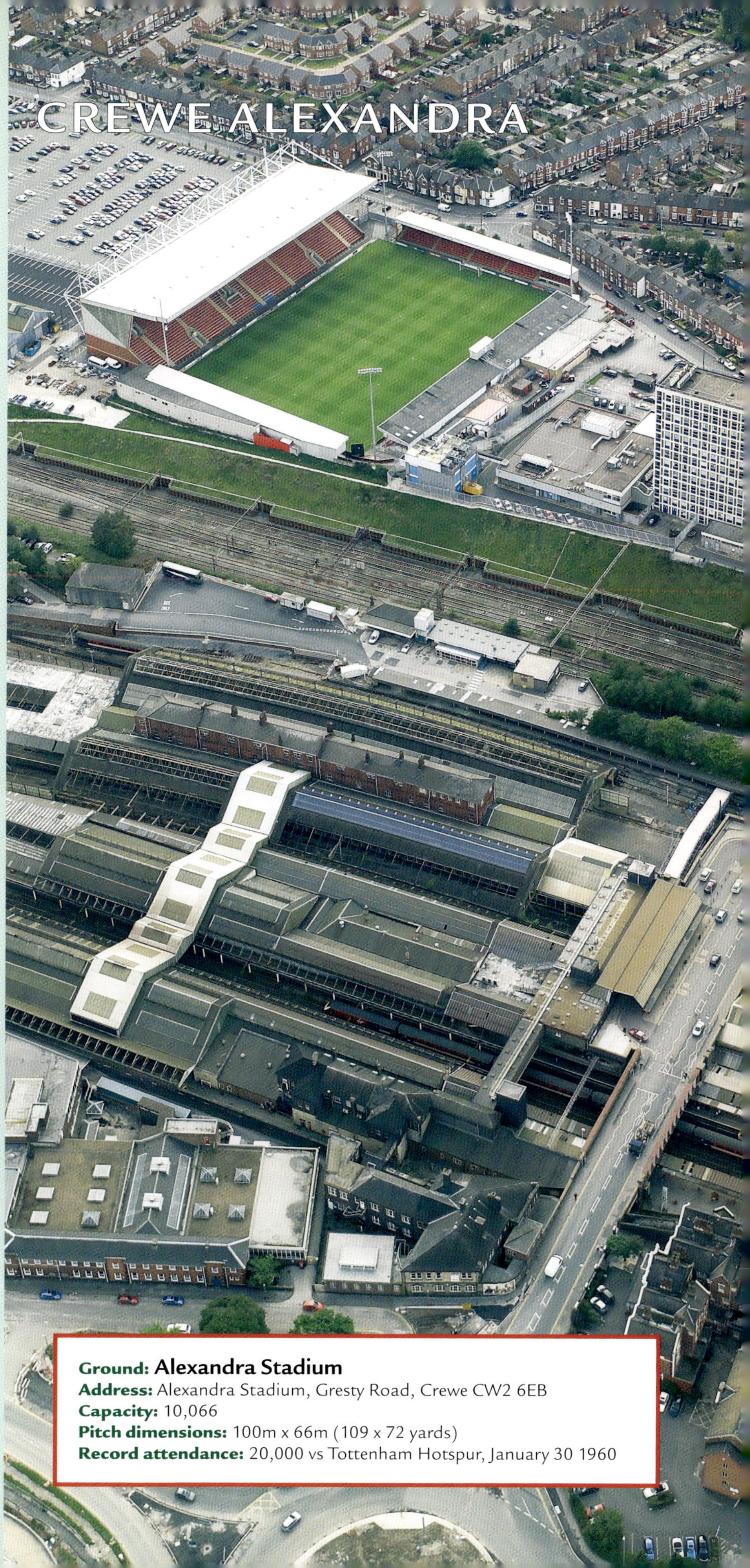

Ground: **Alexandra Stadium**
Address: Alexandra Stadium, Gresty Road, Crewe CW2 6EB
Capacity: 10,066
Pitch dimensions: 100m x 66m (109 x 72 yards)
Record attendance: 20,000 vs Tottenham Hotspur, January 30 1960

COVENTRY CITY

Ground: Ricoh Arena
Address: Ricoh Arena, Phoenix Way, Foleshill, Coventry CV6 6GE
Capacity: 32,500
Pitch dimensions: 105m x 68m (115 x 74 yards)
Record attendance: (at Highfield Road) 51,455 vs Wolverhampton Wanderers, April 29 1967

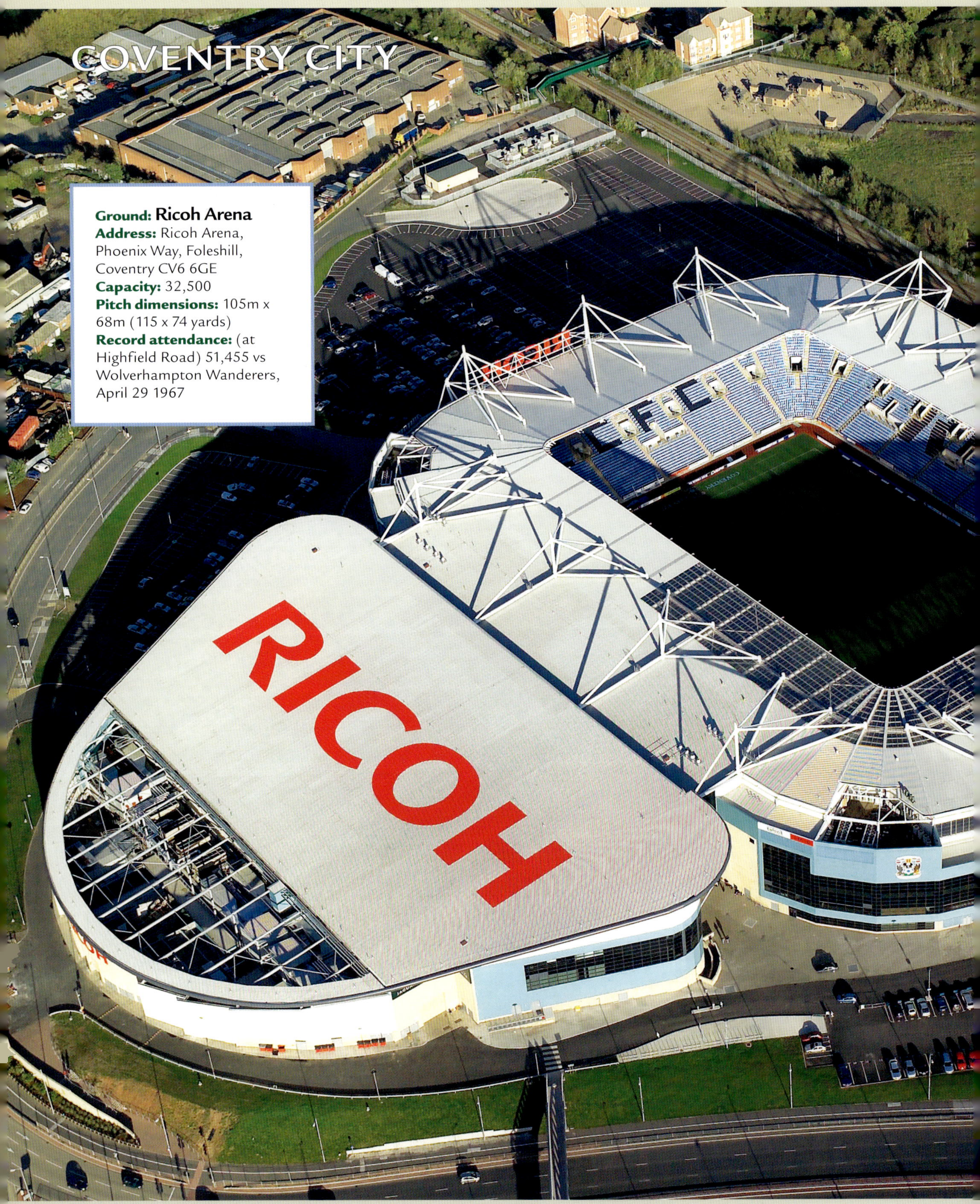

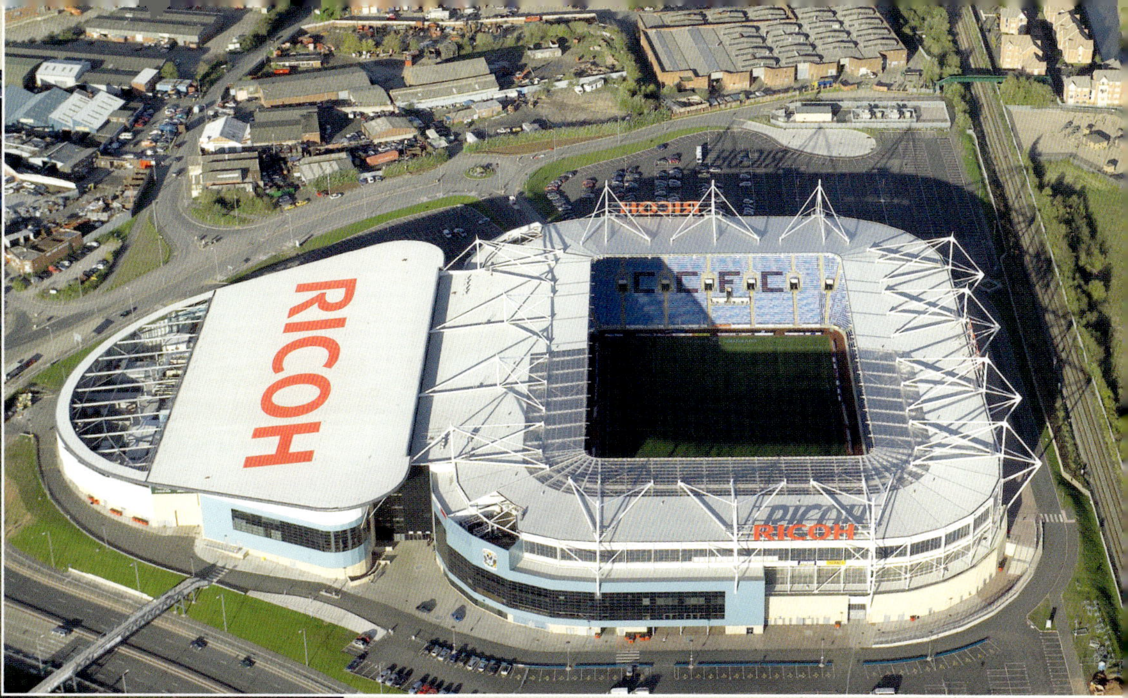

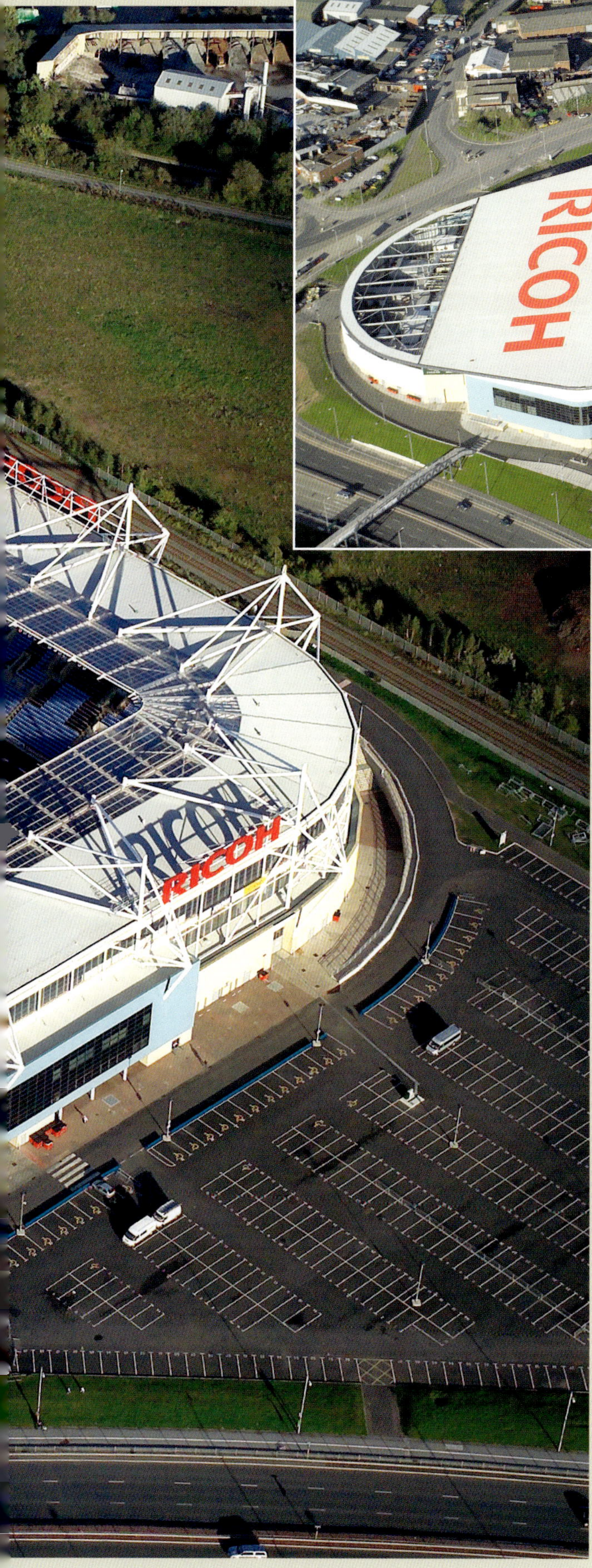

Coventry City FC was founded in 1883 by workers at the local Singer factory, a manufacturer of bicycles. The club played at various grounds before moving to Highfield Road in 1899. City joined the Southern League in 1908 and a good run in the Cup two years later helped to finance a new stand with a roof on the Thackhall Street side. They joined the League in 1919 and further developments were made to the ground, including the erection of the Kop in 1922 and a cover over the West Terrace. The Main Stand was built to replace the original stand on the south side of the pitch, and the club bought Highfield Road outright in 1936. Two years later terracing was extended at the Kop's north corner, known as the Crow's Nest. The ground was not badly hit during the Blitz; the pitch was destroyed but little else was damaged. Jimmy Hill's appointment as manager in 1961 brought in sweeping changes. The club rose from the Third to the First Division in just six years and the ground was developed to reflect this success. The Thackhall Street Stand had seats added and the new Sky Blue Stand was built. With Hill as chairman, more significant changes were introduced. In 1981 Highfield Road became England's first all-seater stadium, but disapproval from fans saw terraces reintroduced a few seasons later. During the 1990s the new all-seater East Stand was built and the Main Stand re-roofed. The 2004-5 season was the club's last at Highfield Road and they have now moved to the 32,500 all-seater Ricoh Arena. This stylish stadium has an unusual Sky Blues' Wall of Fame on the back of the East Stand.

DERBY COUNTY

Players from Derby County Cricket Club formed Derby County FC in 1884. Their first pitch was part of the cricket ground, which was in the middle of a racecourse. Derby soon tired of rescheduling games that clashed with race meetings, and in 1895 they moved to a baseball ground that owner Francis Ley had built after a visit to the US. The Baseball Ground was very enclosed however, and in 1923 Derby received an offer to move to Osmanton Park stadium. They turned this offer down and in 1924 they bought the Baseball Ground from Francis Ley. In 1925 the Popular Side was concreted, and a year later the Rams went back up to the First Division, which funded further ground developments. A two-tiered stand, opened in 1933, was built where the Osmanton Terrace and Catcher's Corner had stood. By the start of WWII all four sides of the Baseball Ground had been rebuilt and covered. The Rams returned to the First Division in 1969 under the management of Brian Clough; this was the same year the Ley Stand opened, and a record 41,826 fans crammed in to see Derby take on Spurs. Crowd trouble in the late 1970s and 1980s saw fences and barriers erected throughout the ground, and calls by local residents for the club to move. In the 1980s the club was struggling under massive debts and they were relegated to the Third Division. These problems were eased when Robert Maxwell took over as chairman in 1984. The fences came down in 1989 and after the Taylor report the club developed plans to rebuild the stadium. They were offered another chance to leave the ground, this time to go to Pride Park. Yet again the club turned the offer down and began working on plans for a 28,000 all-seater Baseball Ground. However, in 1995, after seeing the success of Middlesbrough's relocation they moved to Pride Park. The £16m project took 46 weeks and at the start of the 1997/98 season the Rams began playing at Pride Park, a 33,597 all-seater stadium.

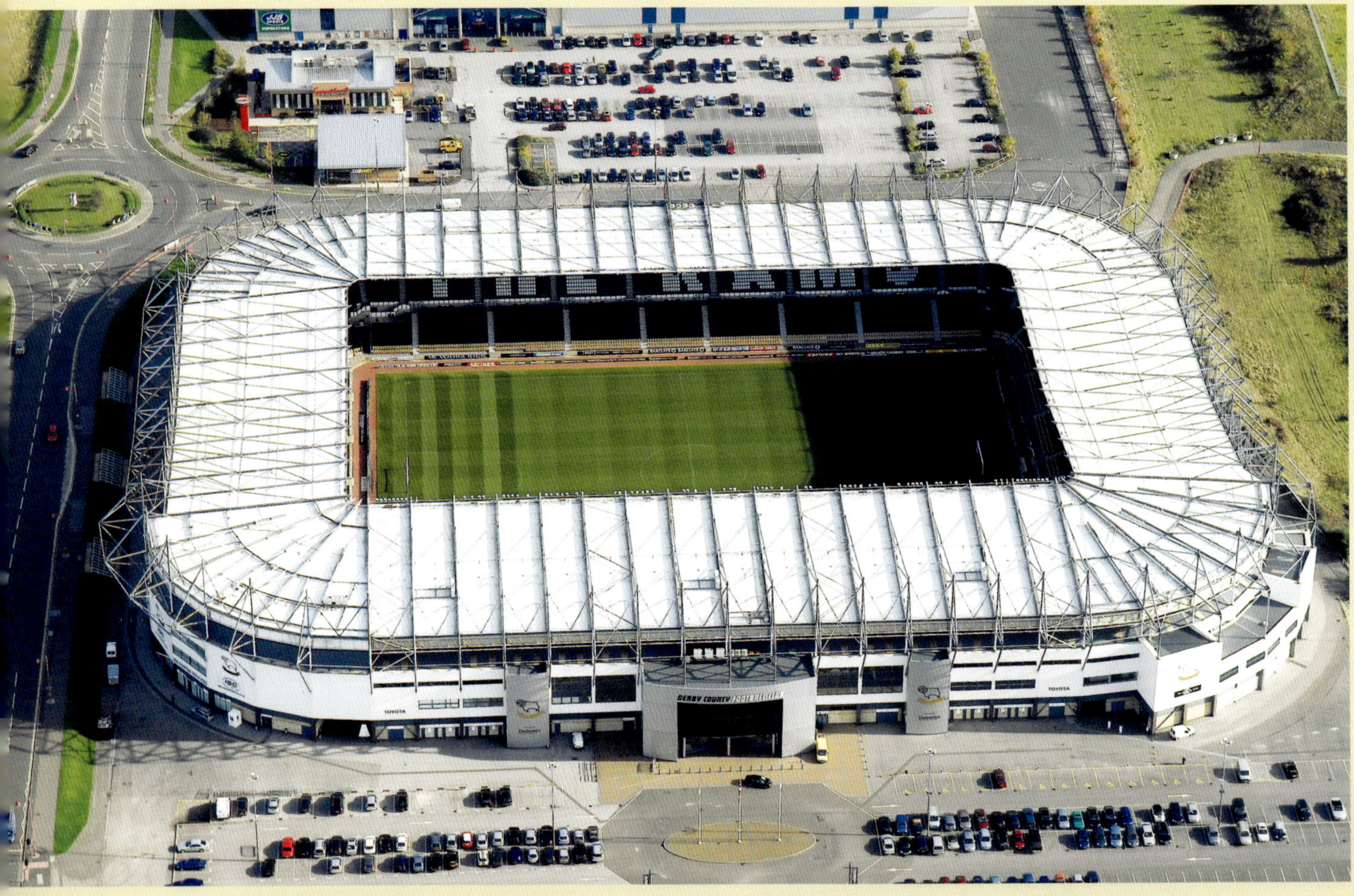

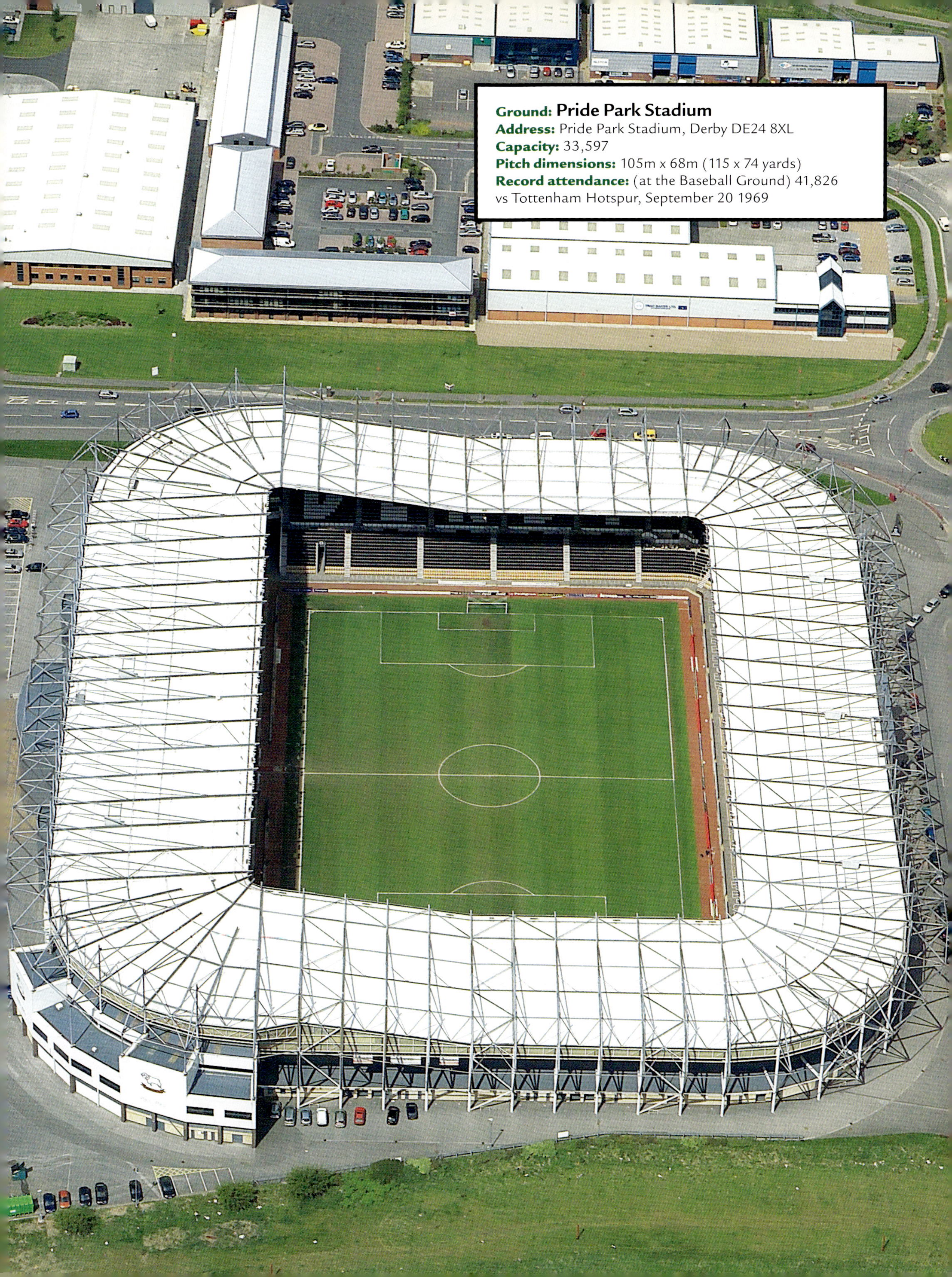

Ground: **Pride Park Stadium**
Address: Pride Park Stadium, Derby DE24 8XL
Capacity: 33,597
Pitch dimensions: 105m x 68m (115 x 74 yards)
Record attendance: (at the Baseball Ground) 41,826 vs Tottenham Hotspur, September 20 1969

IPSWICH TOWN

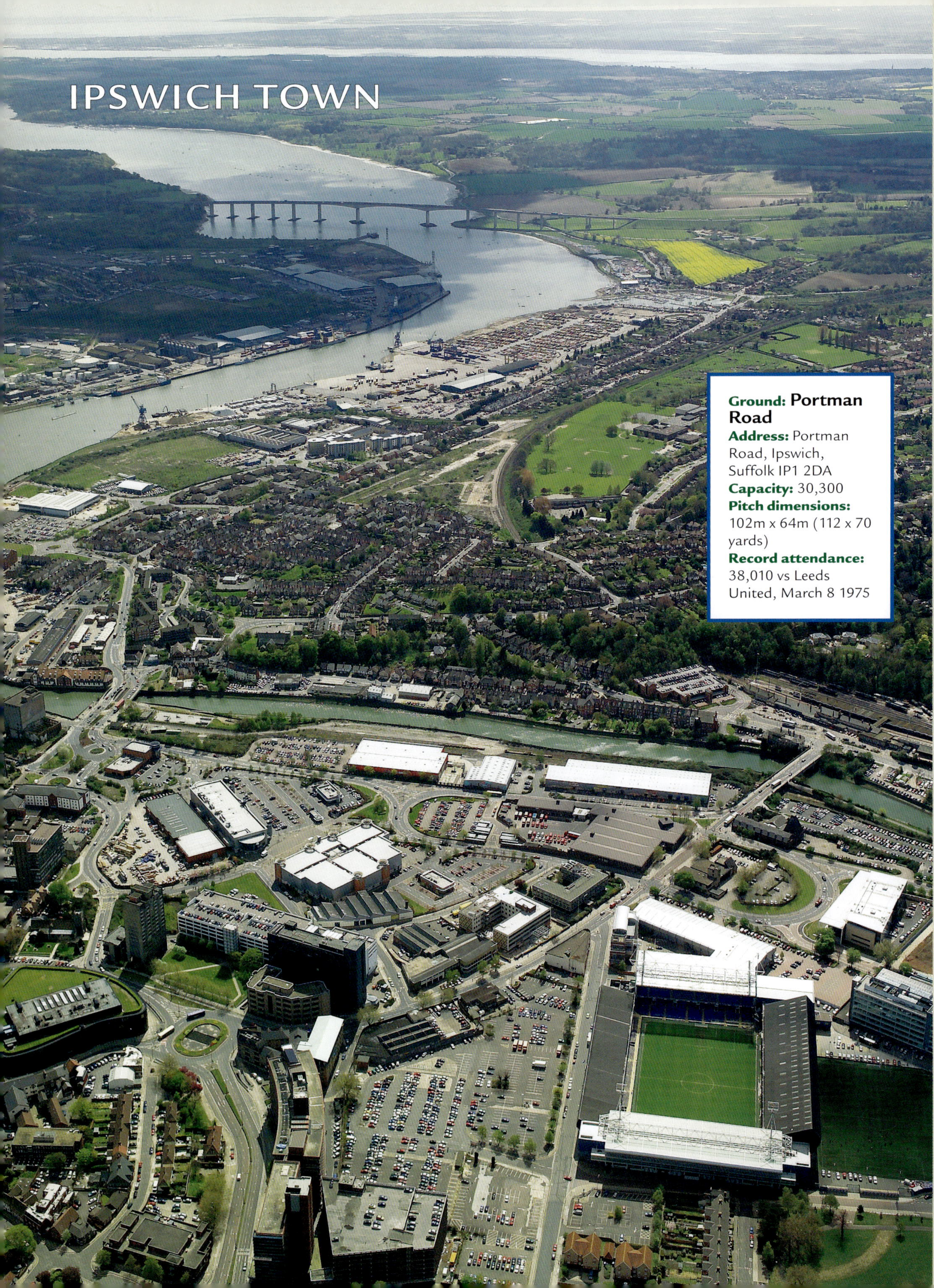

Ground: **Portman Road**
Address: Portman Road, Ipswich, Suffolk IP1 2DA
Capacity: 30,300
Pitch dimensions: 102m x 64m (112 x 70 yards)
Record attendance: 38,010 vs Leeds United, March 8 1975

Ipswich began life as Ipswich AFC in 1878. The club's first ground was on Broom Hill, Norwich Road. In 1888 the football team merged with the local rugby team to become Ipswich Town and they moved to Portman Road, the town's best sporting venue. The rugby team broke away in 1893 but Town continued to share Portman Road with East Suffolk Cricket Club. In 1905 the Ipswich Cricket, Football and Athletic Ground Company formed to pay for separate football and cricket pitches. There was a wooden stand along the Portman Road side but nothing else divided the two pitches. Portman Road suffered damage and neglect when the army took over the ground during the First World War. They refused to leave the ground until 1920, by which time the pitch was ruined. Town eventually turned professional in 1936 but the ground still only had one stand. That summer the club put up fencing and terracing, raising the capacity to 15,000. The following year more terracing was added to the Churchman's End and the club added more seats to the East Stand, both of which were further expanded next season when Ipswich joined the League in 1939. In 1957, under the management of Alf Ramsey, Ipswich was promoted to Division Two. On the basis of this success, they constructed the West Stand, a two-tier stand with a pitched roof. Between 1972-82 Ipswich continued their footballing success under Bobby Robson and the club carried out extensive redevelopments, demolishing the East Stand and replacing it with the Portman Stand. The next major changes took place in the 1980s when the West Stand was extended and renamed the Pioneer Stand. This stand had to be developed just eight years later following the Taylor report when seats were added. Next, seats were installed on both terraces and Portman Road became the first Premier League ground to become all-seater. The developments continued and the Greene King, or South Stand, opened in 2001 and a year later the new North Stand was opened.

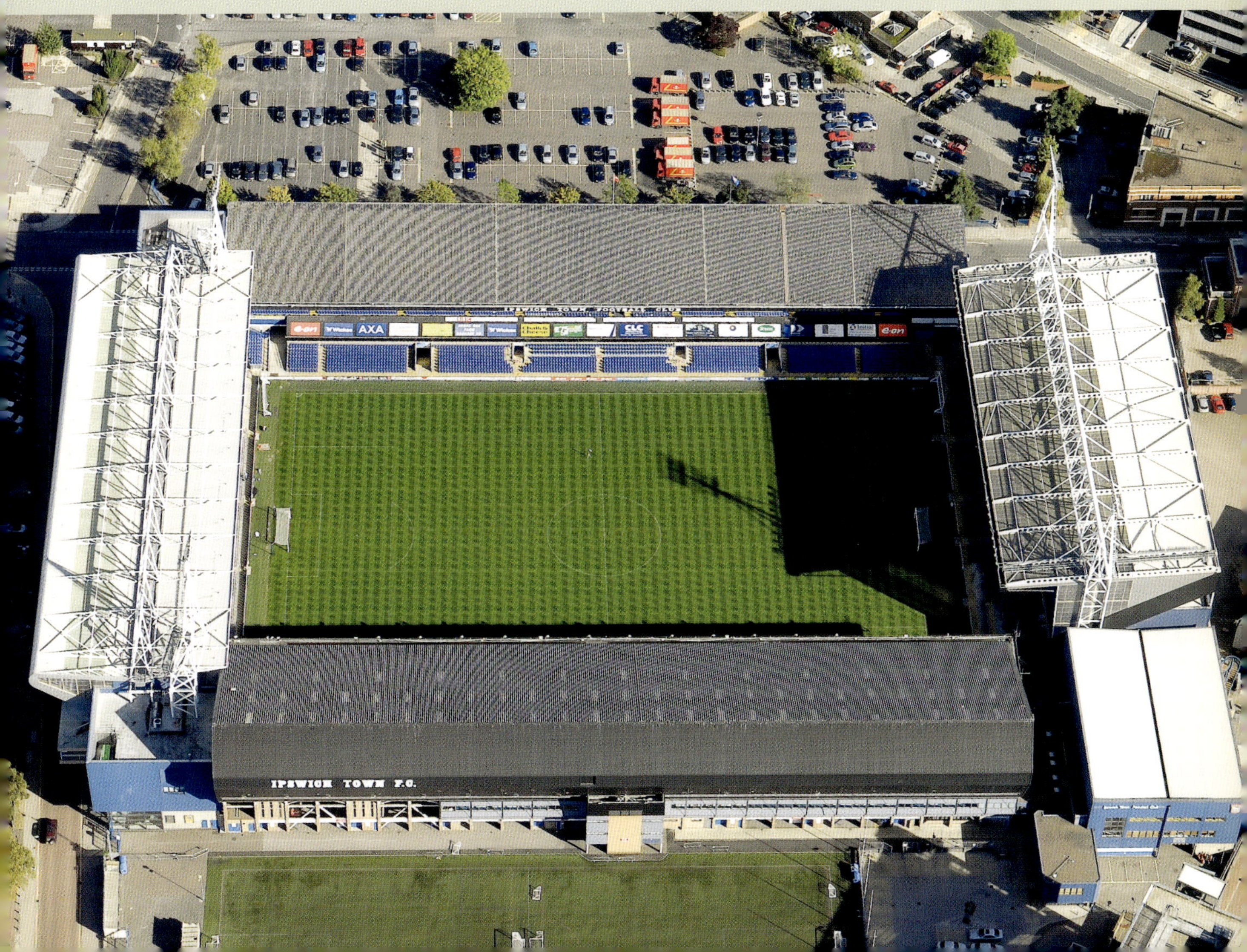

LEICESTER CITY

Many of Leicester City's founder members lived near Fosse Way in the city's west end so it was not surprising that the team was first known as Leicester Fosse when it was established in 1884. In their first year the team played at the racecourse before moving the following year to Victoria Park. In 1889 Leicester turned professional and moved to Mill Lane, which they left two years later when they found a good site at Filbert Street. While the Filbert Street site was being prepared for football, the team played home games at Aylestone Road Cricket Ground. Filbert Street was then known as Walnut Street and the facilities included a low main stand.

It was not until after the First World War that Leicester began major developments of the ground and changed their name to Leicester City. In 1921 the new Main Stand was opened, coming complete with mock classical podium and a very grand players' entrance to the pitch with a small window either side of the players' tunnel and brass rails. In 1927 the club built a two-tier stand at the

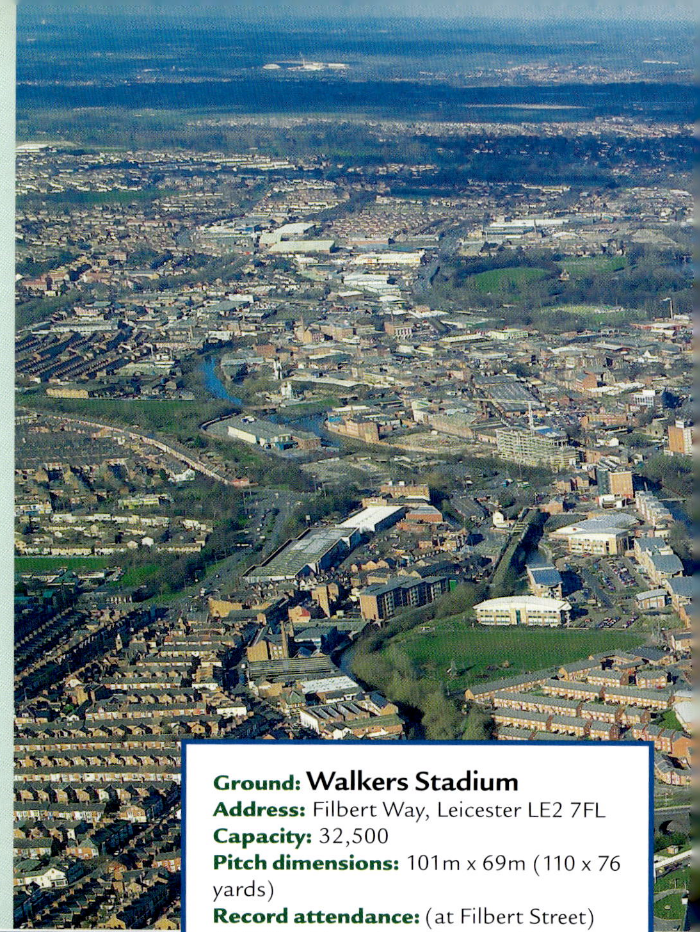

Ground: Walkers Stadium
Address: Filbert Way, Leicester LE2 7FL
Capacity: 32,500
Pitch dimensions: 101m x 69m (110 x 76 yards)
Record attendance: (at Filbert Street) 47,298 vs Tottenham Hotspur, February 18 1928

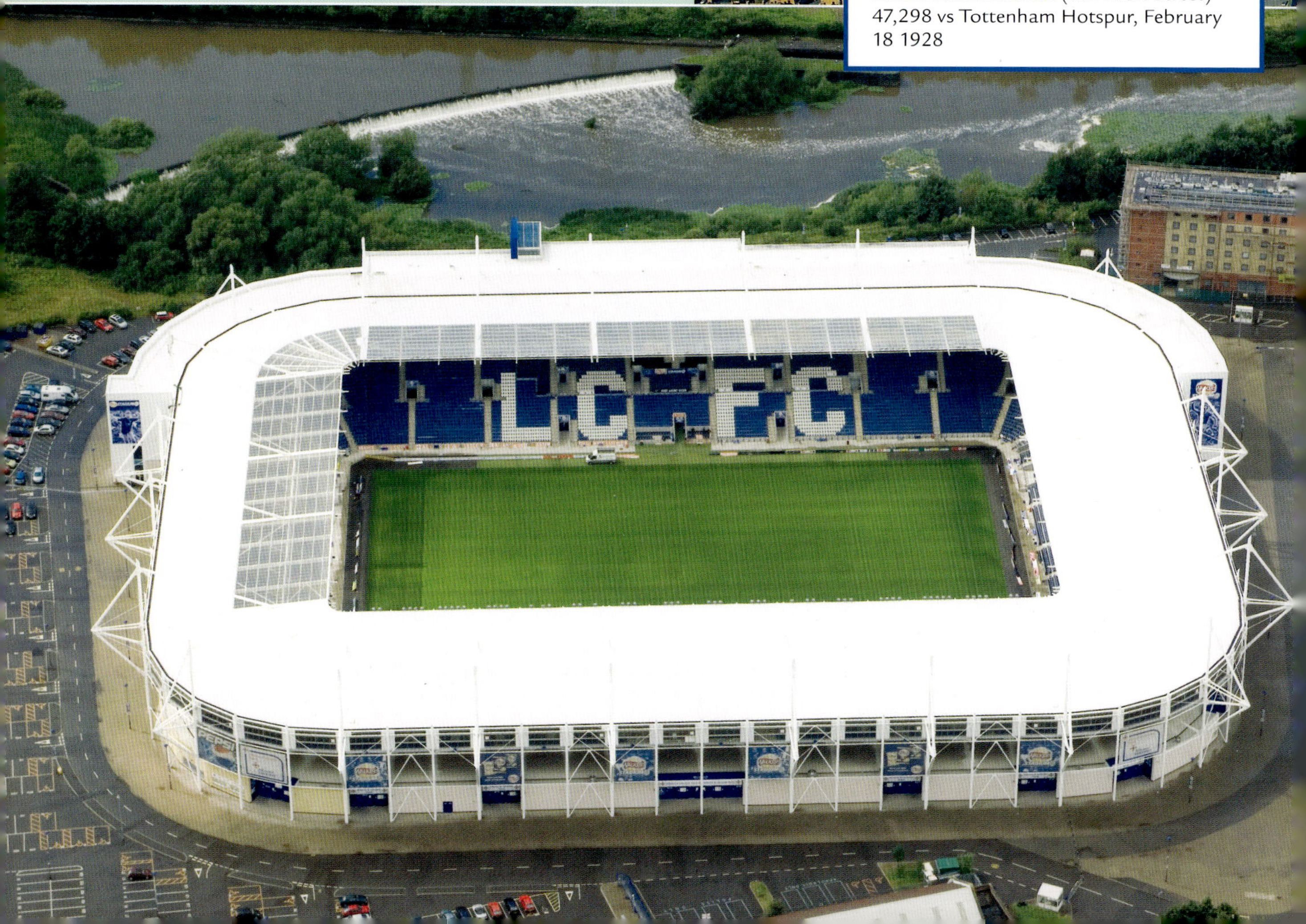

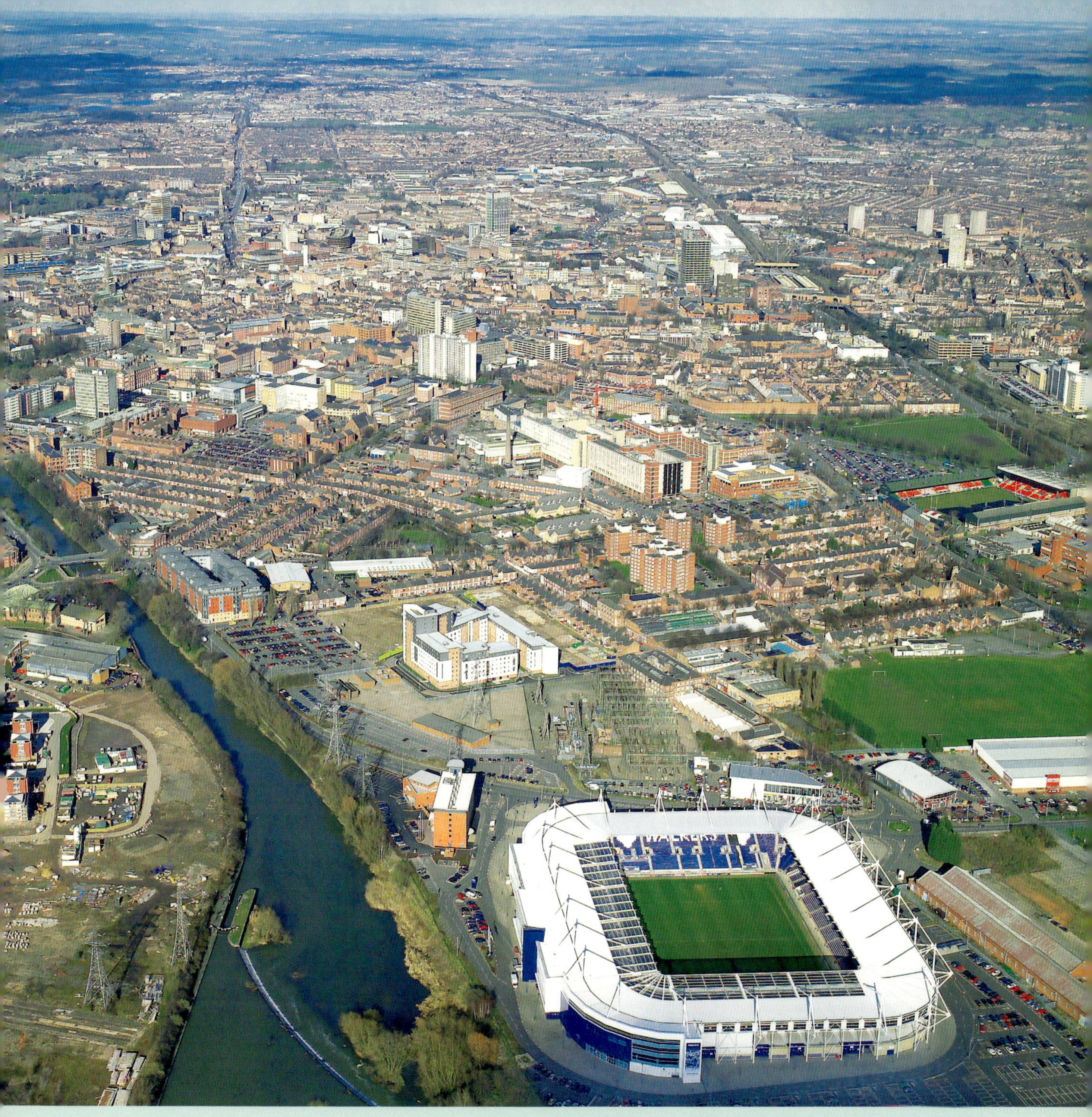

Kop End and moved the Kop to the Filbert Street End. In February 1928, 47,298 fans crammed in to see the Foxes take on Spurs in the FA Cup, the largest-ever crowd at Filbert Street. In the late 1930s, the last remaining open section was covered. The next phase of major development was in the 1970s when the club began converting terraces to seating. The developments started in 1971 with the Filbert Street Terrace, which became the North Stand; next the Popular Side was turned into the all-seater East Stand. The 1990s saw further plans for change, and the club considered either building a completely new stand, or turning the pitch 90°. In the end, they opted to do neither and rebuilt the Main Stand. However, this still provided a cramped ground and in 2002 the club moved to the all-seater Walkers Stadium constructed at a short distance from the Filbert Street ground. The new £35m stadium is completely enclosed, with all sides the same height and style.

LINCOLN CITY

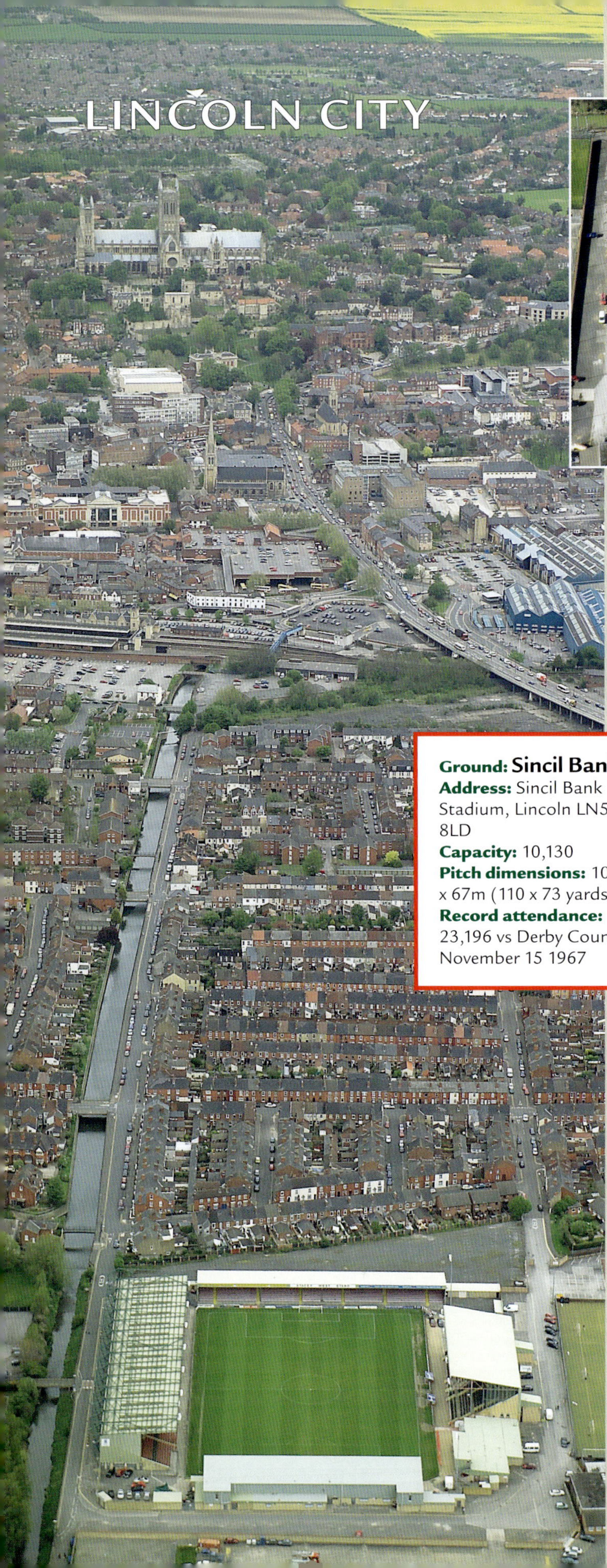

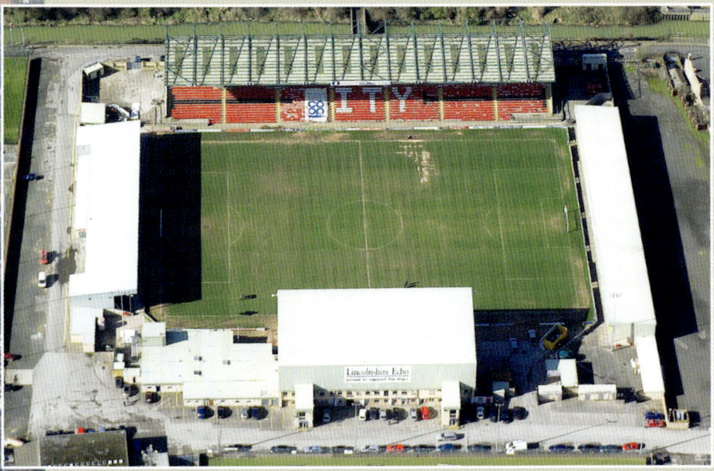

Ground: **Sincil Bank**
Address: Sincil Bank Stadium, Lincoln LN5 8LD
Capacity: 10,130
Pitch dimensions: 101m x 67m (110 x 73 yards)
Record attendance: 23,196 vs Derby County, November 15 1967

Formed in 1884, Lincoln's first matches were played at the John O'Gaunts ground. The club turned professional in the 1891/2 season and, in 1895, moved to their current ground, Sincil Bank. "The Bank" had one small uncovered stand which was built at the South Park End in 1896. Extensive banking was added and in 1899 a covered stand – known as the Working Men's Stand – was erected on the Sincil Bank side. In 1901 the South Park End also got a new stand when the existing stand was moved to the south-east corner. In the 1920s the club added a small shelter at the Railway End and developed the area under the South Park Stand. In September 1929 a fire destroyed the South Park Stand. Within six weeks a new structure with seating for 1,500 spectators was erected in its place. In 1931 terracing was laid on the Railway End. In the following year a new stand at the St Andrews End was erected. In 1948 the Sincil Bank Stand was demolished because of its poor state of repair; the terracing created boosted capacity to 25,000. Floodlighting was installed in 1962 but for the next 20 years the ground remained largely unmodernised and the club fell into financial decay. In 1987 a new stand with a capacity of 1,400 was built at the St Andrews End and in 1990, a new north stand – the Stacey West Stand, named after two revered City fans killed in the Bradford fire – was erected. The new South Park Stand (now known as the IMPS Stand) was completed in 1992 and the EDT Family Stand erected alongside the St Andrews Stand in 1994. The 5,700-seater Linpave Stand (now the Cooperative Community Stand), the first cantilevered stand in the country, replaced the last section of open terracing in 1995. The ground became all-seater in 1999.

LUTON TOWN

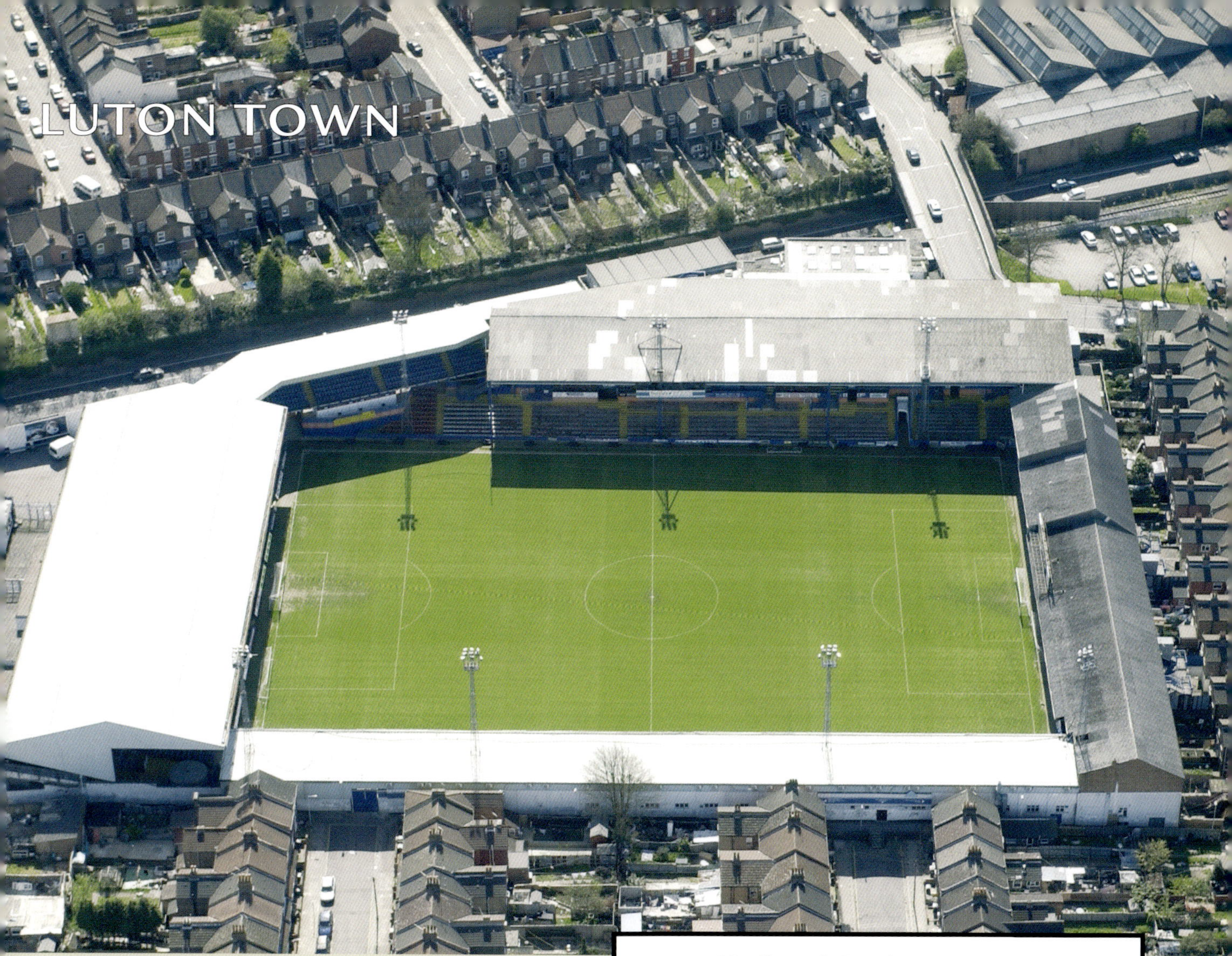

Ground: **Kenilworth Road**
Address: Kenilworth Road Stadium, 1 Maple Road, Luton LU4 8AW
Capacity: 10,300
Pitch dimensions: 101m x 66m (110 x 72 yards)
Record attendance: 30,069 vs Blackpool, March 4 1959

Luton Town formed in 1885 and played their first games at Dallow Lane, where they remained until 1897, when they moved to Dunstable Road. The club stayed at Dunstable Road for eight years before moving again to Kenilworth Road in 1905. A main stand stood along one edge of the pitch, a covered cinder bank stood on the other side and there was banking at each end. The Main Stand burned down in 1921 and was replaced with a stand from Kempton Racecourse. In 1933 the club bought the ground's freehold and paid for a new terrace to be built opposite the Main Stand; this terrace was known as the Bobbers' Stand (as entrance to this stand cost a bob, one old shilling). In 1935 the Oak Road Terrace was covered and two years later the Kenilworth Road End was extended. In 1955 the Oak Road Terrace was also extended and just four years later a record attendance of 30,069 saw the Hatters take on Blackpool in a Cup match. The club experienced mixed fortunes over the next 20 years, falling to the Fourth Division and climbing back up to the First Division. During this time the club took the decision to relocate, although so far all attempts have proved fruitless. Seats were added to the Bobbers Stand in 1979 but in 1985 these were removed and replaced with executive boxes and an artificial pitch was also installed. The executive boxes reduced capacity so much at Kenilworth Road that the club decided to ban all away fans; to help control this, they introduced a membership card scheme for home fans. This did nothing for the atmosphere at Kenilworth Road and in 1991 away fans were allowed back and the artificial pitch was ripped up and replaced. The club still hopes to relocate, and have therefore put any further development of the ground on hold.

MANSFIELD TOWN

The Stags trace their history back to the Wesleyan church on Bridge Street where they started out in 1897 playing under the name of Mansfield Wesleyans. In 1910 they adopted the name Mansfield Town. In 1919 the Stags moved to Field Mill – a ground where football has been played since 1861 making it the second oldest football ground in the UK after Sheffield FC. The club had to share the ground with a local cricket team, who owned the only building on site – a cricket pavilion. The cricketers were not keen on sharing the building, however, and Stag's players had to change in the nearby Brown Cow pub. In 1921 the Duke of Portland sold the land to Mansfield Town and turnstiles were erected at both the North and Quarry Ends. Ash and waste from nearby coalpits were used to build up banking and by 1926 the club had terraces on three sides and a covered stand on the west side. Following a good cup run, the Stags built a stand on the Bishop Street side in 1929. Little further development took place until the 1950s when the club bought land adjacent to the west of the ground and the supporter's club funded the building of the North Stand complete with its famous clock in 1957. In 1962 floodlights were installed. When the Hurst Park racecourse in Surrey closed in 1961, the supporter's club paid £10,000 to buy one of their grandstands. It was erected on the west side of the ground in 1966 at a cost of £200,000 – more than six times the original estimate! Following the Taylor report, Mansfield closed the Bishop Street Stand but by the 1990s long-awaited improvements to the ground finally came to fruition with new roofs for the West Stand in 1991 and for the Bishop Street Stand in 1994. In 1999 the North Stand and the Quarry Land End were both demolished and new stands erected in their place in 2000. Finally the West Stand was demolished and replaced by a two-tier stand officially opened in July 2001.

Ground: Field Mill
Address: Quarry Lane, Mansfield NG18 5DA
Capacity: 10,000
Record attendance: 24,467 vs Nottingham Forest, January 10 1953

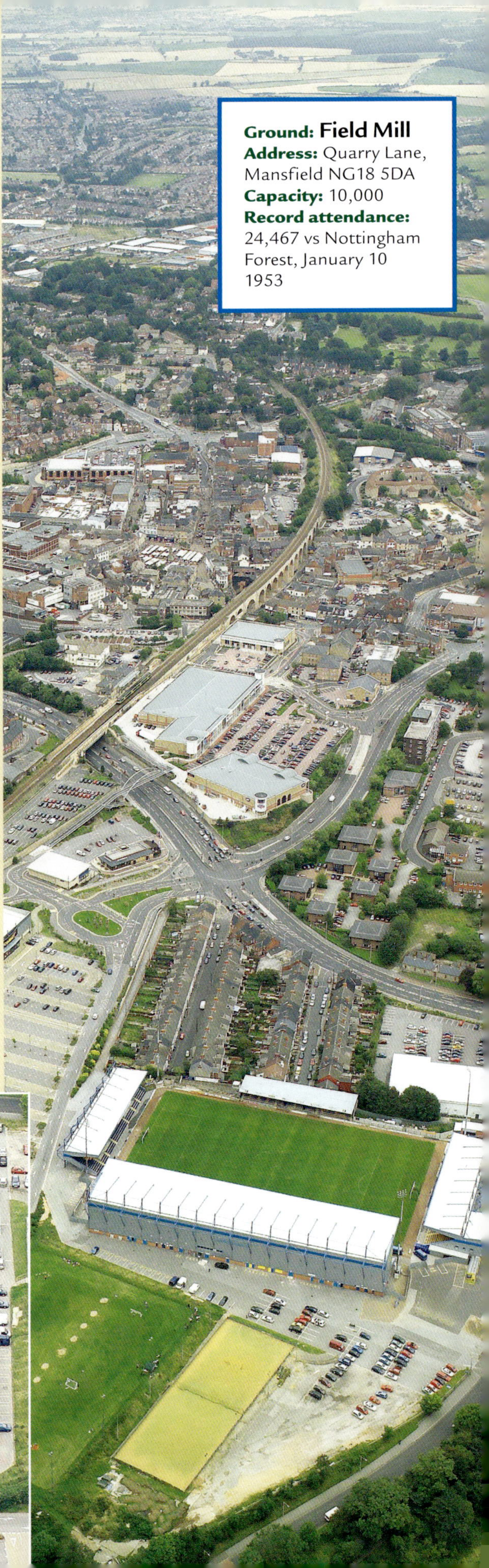

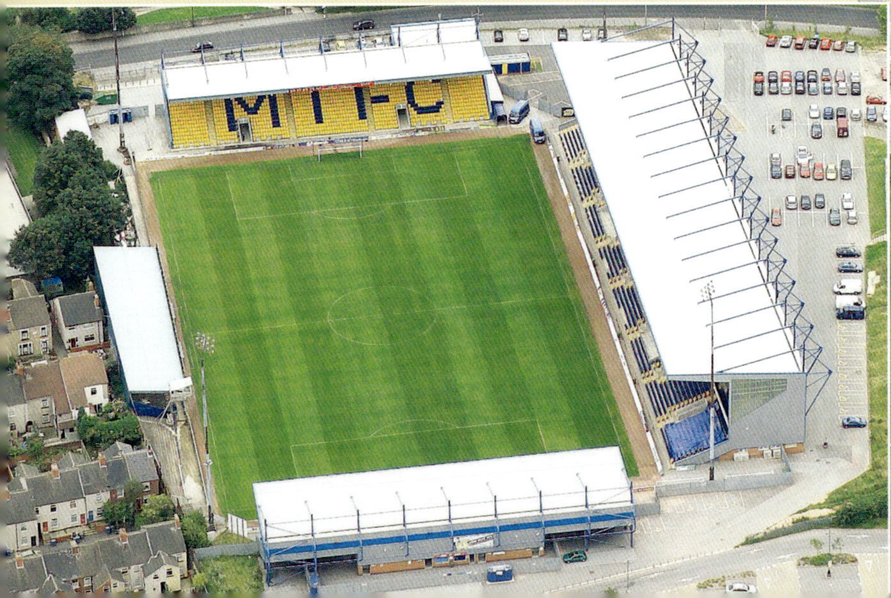

MILTON KEYNES DONS

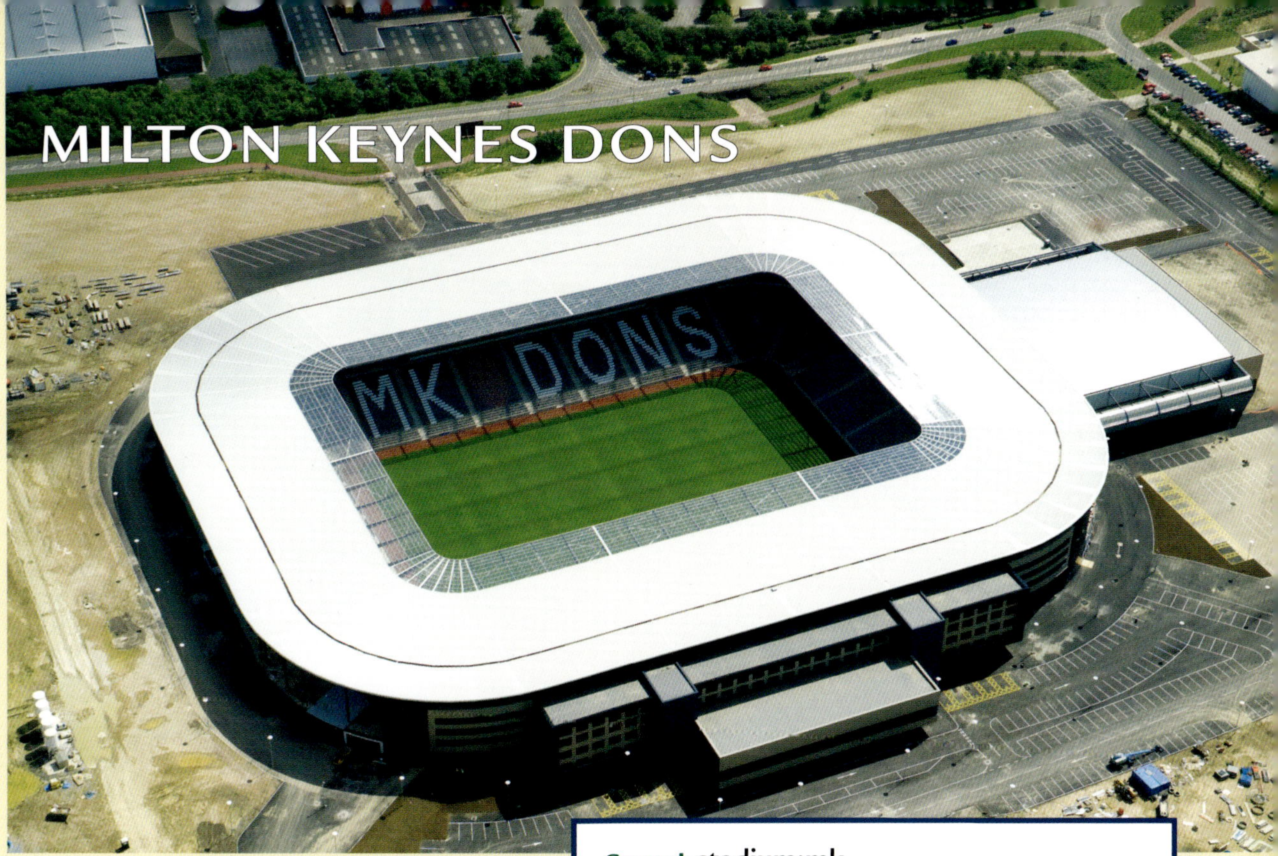

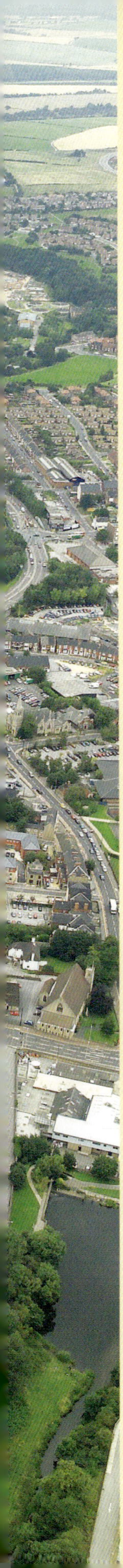

Ground: **stadium:mk**
Address: Stadium Way West, Milton Keynes MK1 1ST
Capacity: 22,000
Record attendance: (at Plough Lane) 18,080 vs HMS Victory, March 2 1935
Record attendance: (at stadium:mk)13.037 vs Lincoln City, October 14 2007

Wimbledon FC formed in 1889 and played their early games on local parks. After merging with Wimbledon Borough in 1912, the club moved to Plough Lane, the site of a former refuse tip. The club bought the South Stand from Clapton Orient in 1923, erected a stand along the north side of the pitch, a terrace on the east side and banking to the west. The South Stand suffered bomb damage during the Second World War but the stand was repaired and it was used until the Dons left Plough Lane in 1991. In 1959 the Main Stand was built along the north side after the club bought the ground from the local council. In 1960 the club added a cover to the West Stand and concreted the terracing. After winning the Amateur Cup in 1963, Wimbledon FC turned professional but it was another 14 years before they managed to join the Football League. Once they did, achievements on the pitch were quick to follow: they reached the First Division in 1986, and won the FA Cup in 1988. Despite the team's meteoric success, in 1990 Plough Lane only had 2,050 seats and, following the Taylor report, could not meet the minimum standards required of a First Division football ground. In 1991 the club bade farewell to Plough Lane and entered into a ground-sharing agreement with Crystal Palace. Plough Lane was still used for reserve team games until 2002, when it was finally demolished. The Dons finally found a new home in Milton Keynes in 2003, at the National Hockey Stadium. Built in the 1990s it has a single-tiered main stand on the south side, an uncovered stand opposite and two temporary stands at either end. Despite stiff resistance from some fans, the club changed its name to Milton Keynes Dons at the start of the 2004/05 season.

At the beginning of the 2007 season, the Dons moved to the spectacular new stadium:mk in the Denbigh district of the town. Construction of the new stadium began in February 2005 and it will eventually seat 32,000 spectators, although it is likely that the Dons will use only the lower tier of stadium seating with a capacity of 22,000. The stadium will host a number of different sports and is also the home of the Milton Keynes Lions basketball team.

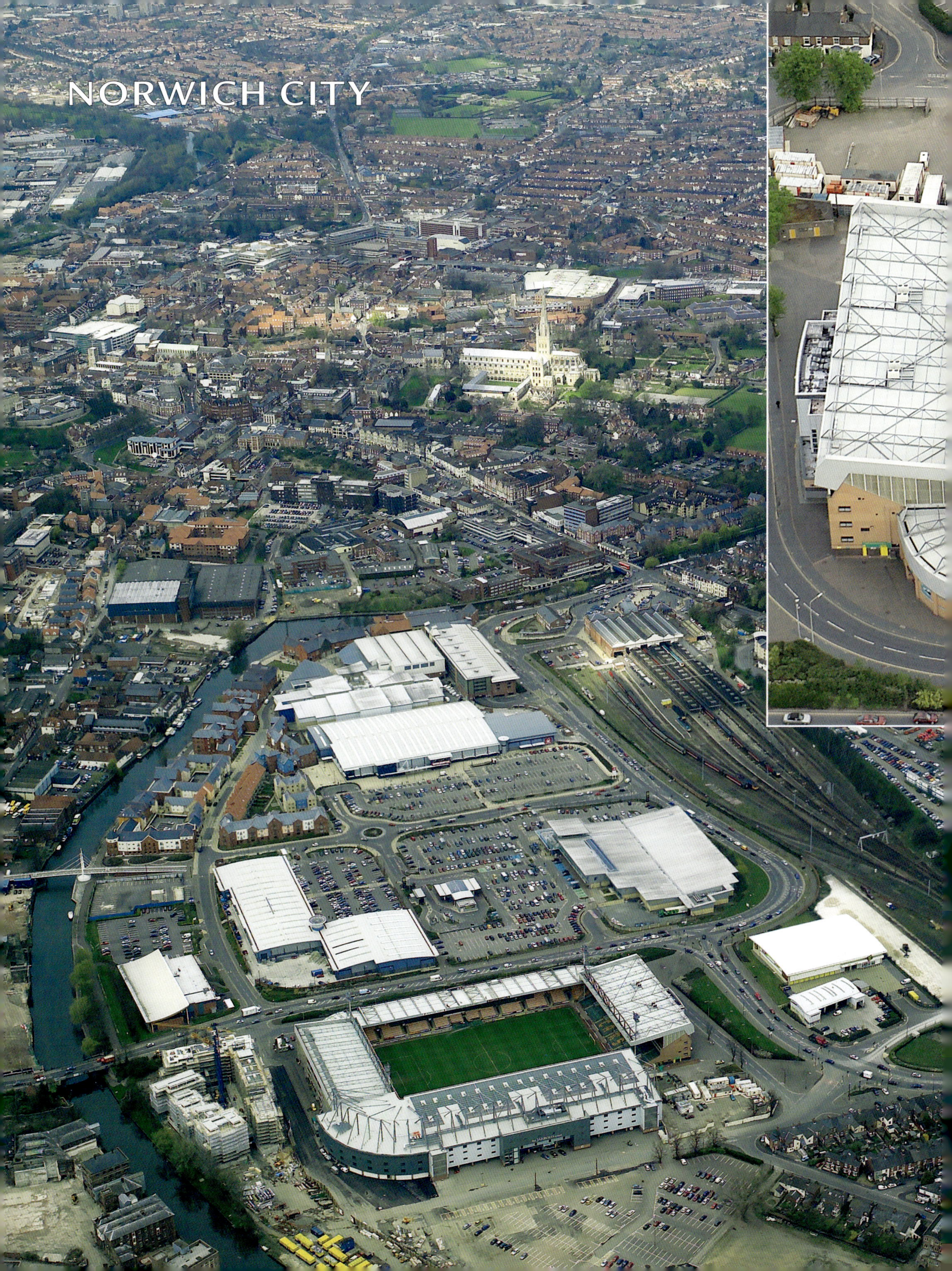
NORWICH CITY

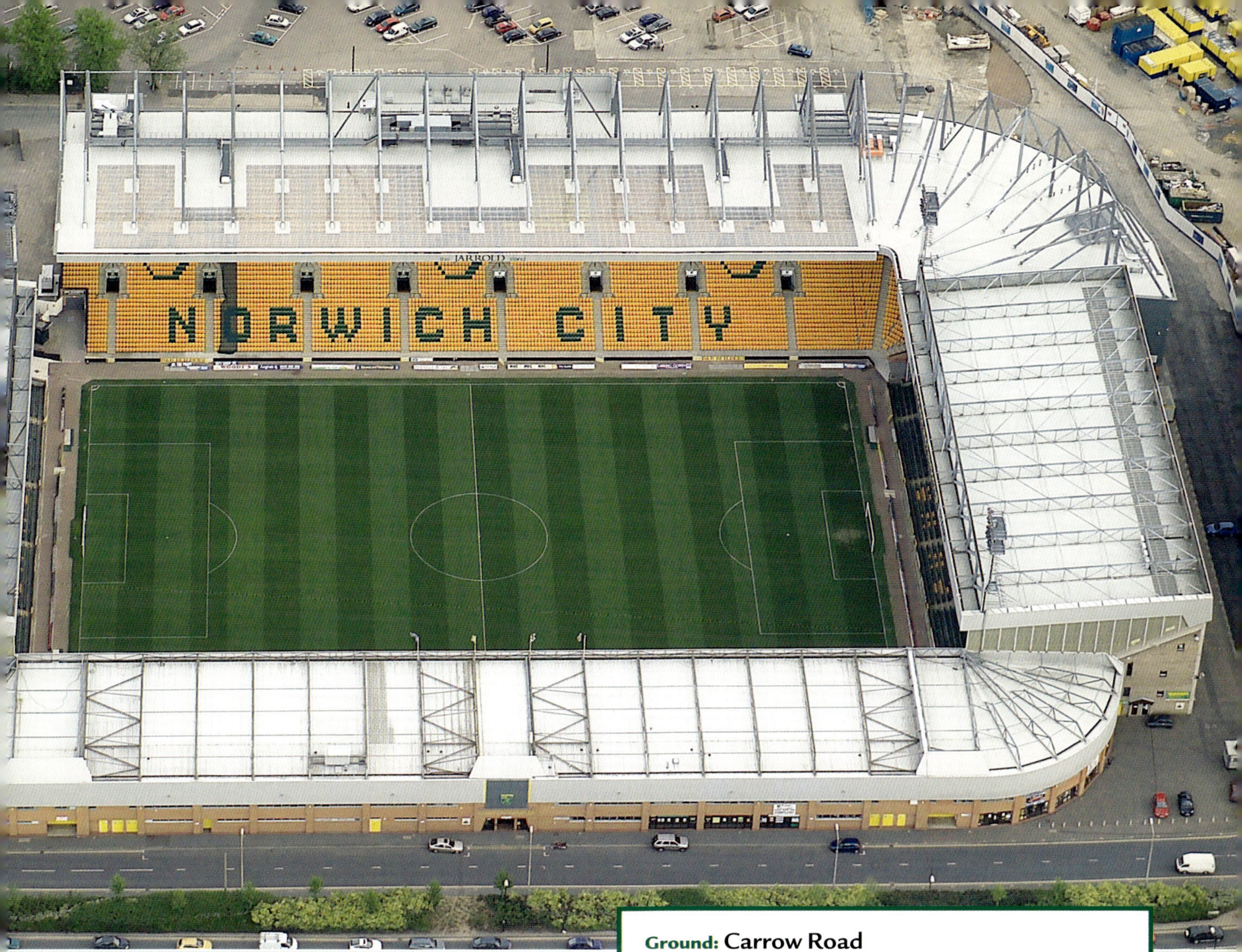

Ground: **Carrow Road**
Address: Carrow Road, Norwich NR1 1JE
Capacity: 26,034
Pitch dimensions: 101m x 69m (114 x 74 yards)
Record attendance: 43,984 vs Leicester City, March 30 1963

Football has been played in Norwich since 1868 but Norwich City did not form until 1902. Their first ground on Newmarket Road belonged to the Norfolk County FA. The Canaries turned professional in 1905, yet there were problems with the rented ground. Their chairman, John Pyke, thought he had solved these when he bought a disused chalkpit on Rosary Road. A wooden stand was brought with the club to the new ground, which labourers spent the summer of 1908 preparing for football. The ground was named the Nest but it was not a particularly suitable home for the Canaries as houses were very close to the pitch at the west end and there was a steep concrete verge at the east end. In 1922 barriers on top of the verge collapsed and a boy was badly injured. Despite these problems, the club continued to play on the ground until 1935. That year the club moved to Carrow Road, a sports ground owned by Colman's Mustard. In just 82 days the club built a 3,500-seater main stand and paddock on one side and embankments on the other three sides. In 1937 the first terrace cover went up at the Station End, renamed the Barclay End, but it was not until 1959, when the Canaries reached the semi-finals of the FA Cup and won promotion, that they could afford further ground improvements. The terrace opposite the Main Stand was covered and in 1963 the South Stand was built. Fire destroyed the central section of the Main Stand in October 1984, which was replaced the following season. The 1990s saw the ground almost completely rebuilt, with new stands on each side. The most recent is the Jarrold Road South Stand which opened in 2004; this can hold 8,000 fans. There are two-tiered stands at either end and the Geoffrey Watling City Stand is a smaller single-tiered stand. The total capacity of the ground is now 26,034.

NOTTS COUNTY

Notts County formed in 1862 and is the oldest club that still plays in the Football League. The team played early games at the Meadows Cricket Ground before moving to Trent Bridge Cricket Ground in 1882. Trent Bridge had a pavilion and the club added a stand along the west side of the pitch. Despite enjoying playing at Trent Bridge, the ground-sharing arrangement was not without its problems as the football team had to find an alternative venue for home games during the cricket season. The club eventually opted to move to Meadow Lane in 1910. Along one side of the ground was a stream, Tinkers Brook. It was on this side that the first cover was added; the Main Stand was built opposite in 1910. There was an embankment at the west end and the club brought the stand they had built at Trent Bridge and installed it at the east end. It was not until 1925 that any new structures were built. That year a new stand, the County Road Stand, was built on the Tinkers Brook side. The Main Stand was damaged during the Second World War but this was repaired in time for Meadow Lane's highest-ever recorded attendance of 47,310 when the Magpies took on York City in the FA Cup in 1955. The following years saw the team sink to the Fourth Division and then rise up to the First Division in 1981. The oldest stand, which the club had brought from Trent Bridge, was finally demolished in 1978 following new safety regulations. The 1990s saw a complete renovation of Meadow Lane, making it an all-seater stadium. In 1992 stands were built at either end and along the north side. In 1994 the new Main Stand was built bringing the capacity of the ground up to 20,300.

Ground: **Meadow Lane**
Address: Meadow Lane, Nottingham NG2 3HJ
Capacity: 20,300
Pitch dimensions: 104m x 69m (114 x 76 yards)
Record attendance: 47,310 vs York City, March 12 1955

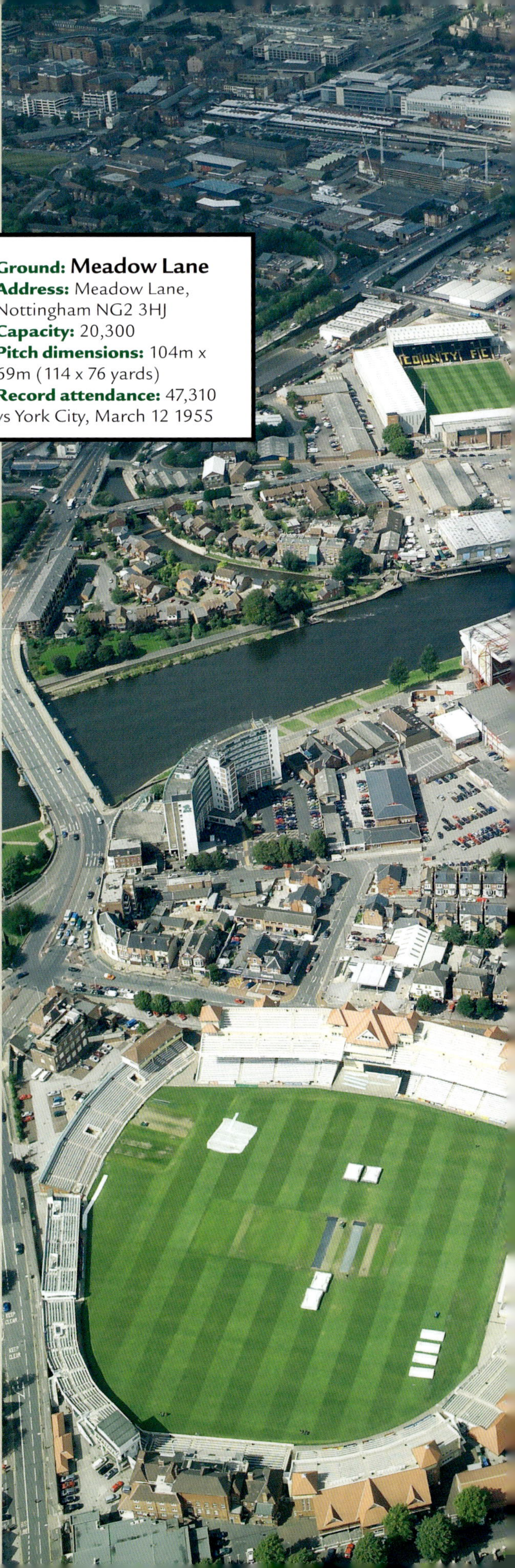

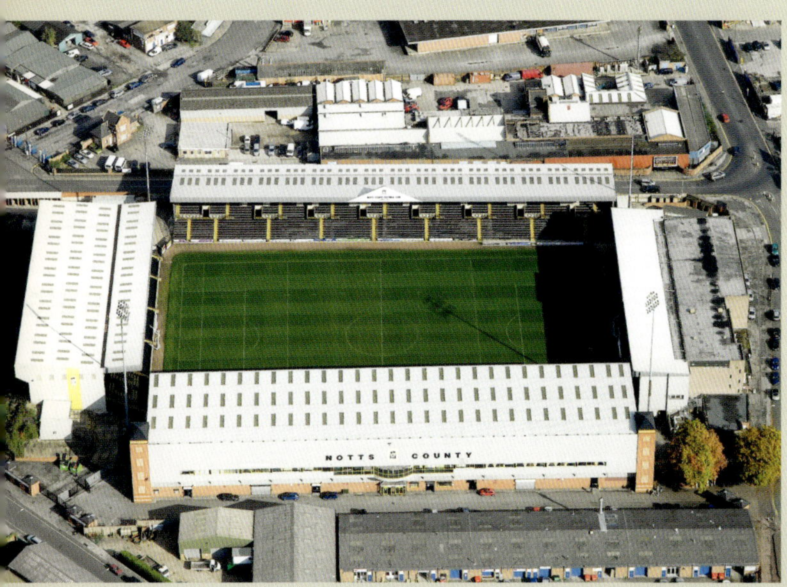

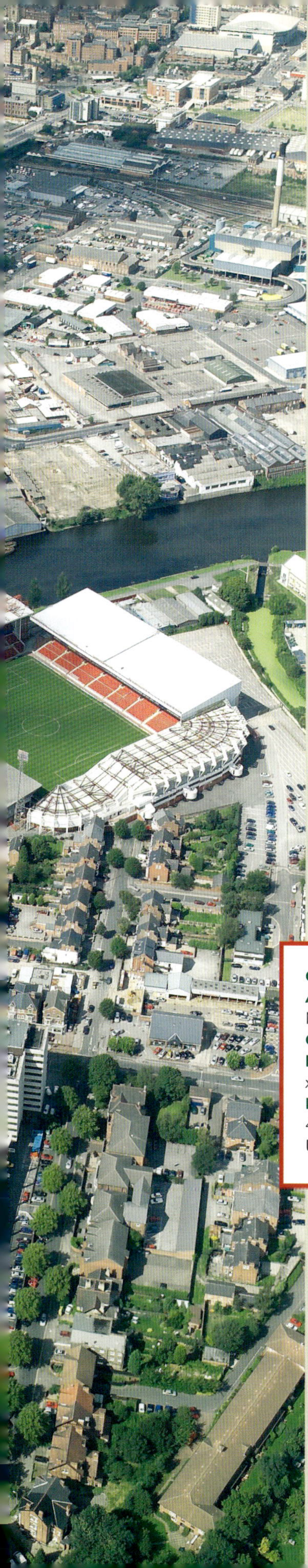

NOTTINGHAM FOREST

Nottingham Forest was formed in 1865 and the club played their first games at the Forest Recreation Ground. They moved in 1879 to the Meadows and just a year later moved on to Trent Bridge, the cricket ground. The club then had a number of different homes and it was not until 1890 that they settled for a while at the Town Ground. It cost the club £1,000 to prepare the ground for football. Forest joined the League in 1892 and in 1898 won their first FA Cup final. This success brought increased numbers of supporters and that year the Reds moved to the City Ground, spending £3,000 on getting it up to scratch. The club built a wooden main stand and a wooden shelter at the Trent End. The City Ground survived the war with very little damage – repairing the ground when the Trent burst its banks in 1947 was more costly. After winning the Third Division title in 1950 they drew up plans for redevelopment. In 1954 the Trent End Terrace was extended and covered, and three years later the club built the East Stand and expanded the Bridgford End Terrace. Between 1962-65 the Main Stand was redeveloped, in time for Forest's highest gate ever when 49,946 fans saw them take on Manchester United in 1967. The following season fire engulfed the Main Stand in a game against Leeds United – fortunately, no fans were injured. The club had to make a temporary move to Meadow Lane, Notts County's ground, for six games while the City Ground was repaired. The late 1970s saw Forest win the League title, the European Cup and the League Cup twice in successive seasons. The money earned from this success funded the building of the two-tiered, all-seater Executive Stand (now called the Brian Clough Stand) in place of the East Stand, at a cost of a cool £2.5m. After a wrangle with the local council over a strip of land behind the Trent End, Forest began developing the Bridgford End in 1992, followed shortly afterwards by the Trent End which brought the capacity up to 30,602. The club's current plans include redevelopment of the Main Stand.

Ground: **City Ground**
Address: City Ground, Nottingham NG2 5FJ
Capacity: 30,602
Pitch dimensions: 105m x 68m (115 x 78 yards)
Record attendance: 49,946 vs Manchester United, October 28 1967

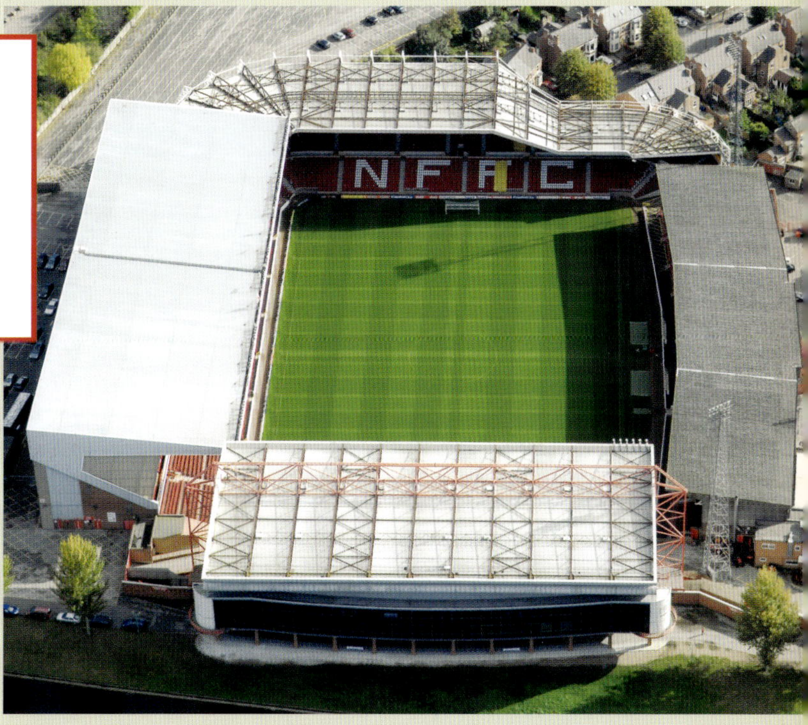

Left: Nottingham's three major sports grounds – Meadow Lane (top), the City Ground (centre) and Trent Bridge, home of Nottingham County Cricket (foreground)

PETERBOROUGH UNITED

Peterborough United was founded in 1934 and evolved from a club called Fletton United, founded in 1923. Fletton already had the nickname Posh, so when Peterborough formed, the nickname stuck. The club's home ground, London Road, was home to a number of football teams before the Posh moved in. In the early days the ground had only one stand, on the north side of the ground, which had 400 seats. In the 1950s major developments at London Road took place: covers were added to either end of the ground and the Main Stand, which took three years to build, opened in 1958 when the original stand was demolished. The south side also had terracing laid during the 1950s. In 1960 Peterborough's success on the pitch saw them join the Fourth Division of the Football League. The following season they were promoted to the Third Division after finishing as champions. Three years later a record attendance of 30,096 saw Peterborough take on Swansea Town and reach the quarter-finals of the FA Cup. The terraces along the sides of the pitch were extended, but then the club's momentum faltered. The team's performances began to slide and the development of London Road ceased completely. It was not until the 1990s that any further improvements to the ground took place. The paddock of the Main Stand had seats added in 1993 in time to meet the new safety regulations required by the Taylor report. In 1996 a new two-tiered stand was built along the south side of the pitch, bringing total capacity at London Road up to 15,314.

Ground: **London Road**
Address: London Road, Peterborough PE2 8AL
Capacity: 15,314
Pitch dimensions: 102m x 69m (112 x 76 yards)
Record attendance: 30,096 vs Swansea Town, February 20 1965

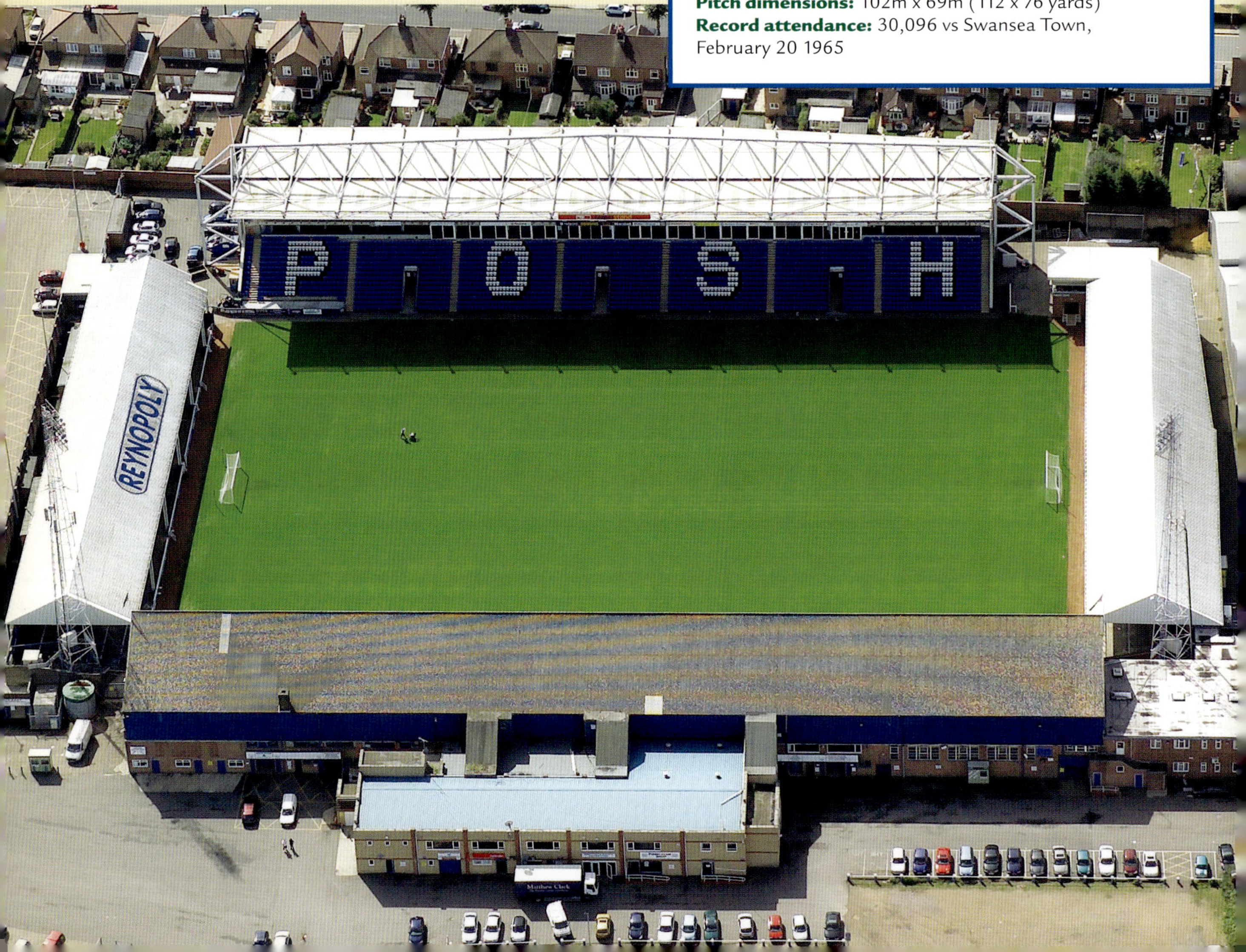

PORT VALE

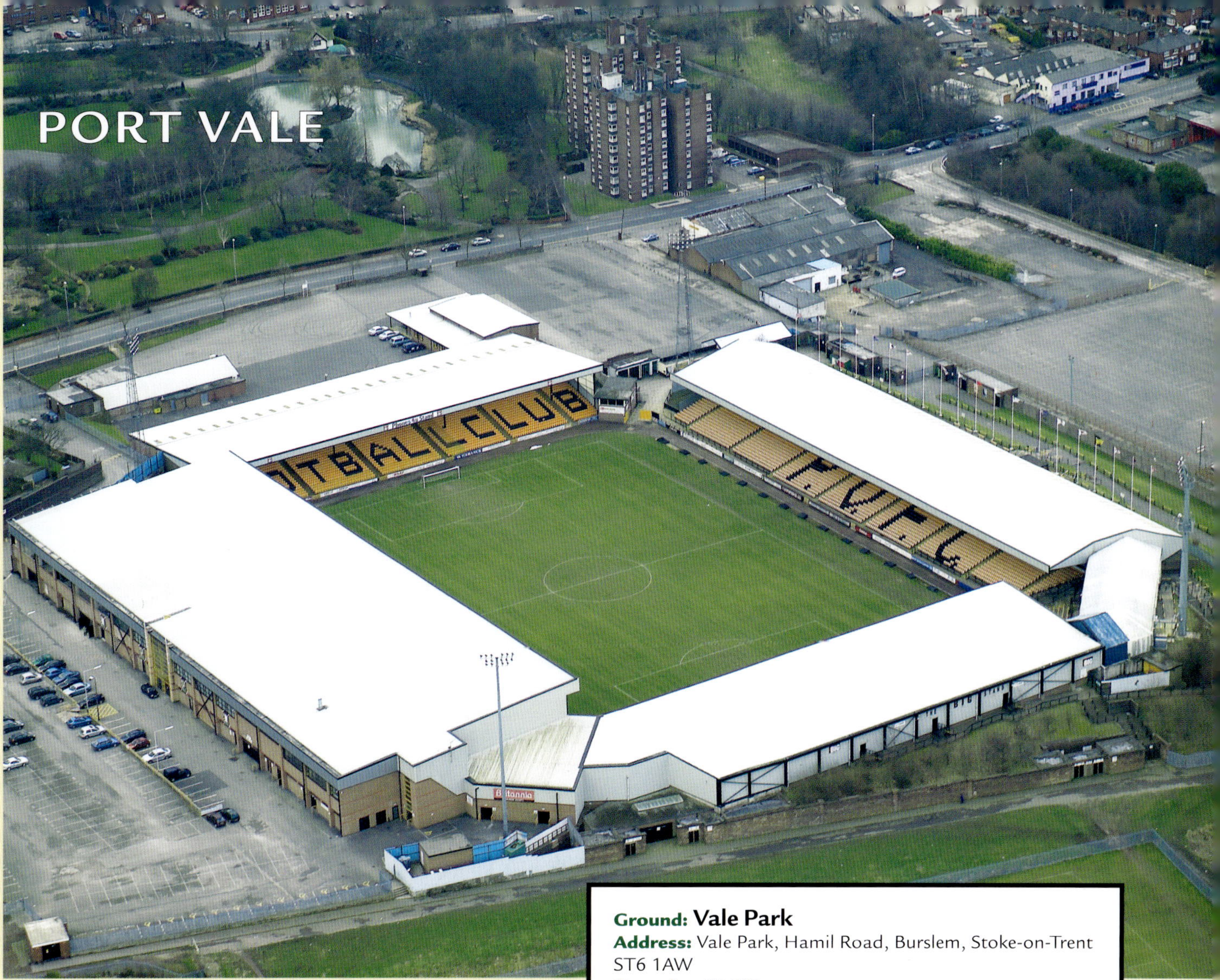

Ground: **Vale Park**
Address: Vale Park, Hamil Road, Burslem, Stoke-on-Trent ST6 1AW
Capacity: 18,392
Pitch dimensions: 104m x 70m (114 x 77 yards)
Record attendance: 49,768 vs Aston Villa, February 20 1960

Opinions vary as to the exact formation date of Port Vale although the club badge states that it was 1876. The Valiants played at various grounds in their early days including a ground close to Burslem station when they adopted the name Burslem Port Vale and turned professional in 1885. The following year the club moved to the Cobridge Athletic Grounds. Financial insolvency threatened in 1896, and despite a hard fight the club were declared bankrupt in 1907. A church team re-formed the club as Port Vale and in 1913 they moved to the Old Recreation Ground where they remained for almost 40 years. After joining the League in 1919, the team bought the ground's freehold. However after the Second World War the club realised they needed a bigger ground and in 1950 they moved in to Vale Park. The ground had terracing on three sides but was completely uncovered. A few months after Vale Park opened, a roof was added to the north end of the ground.

A new stand was built along the west side in 1954 and floodlights were installed four years later. Terracing was added to the north end of the ground in 1959 and the following season Vale Park recorded its highest ever attendance of 49,768 when the Valiants took on Aston Villa in the FA Cup. Very little changed at Vale Park until the 1990s. However, events off the pitch saw Port Vale expelled from the League for financial irregularity in 1968, although they were allowed to rejoin, albeit in the Fourth Division, a season later. In 1991 seats were installed along the west side and a roof was added to the south end. A new cover and seats were added to the north end and stands were added to two of the ground's corners. The Main Stand was finally opened in 2001 and current capacity at Vale Park is 18,392.

STOKE CITY

Stoke City trace their history back to 1863. They were formed from Stoke Ramblers and after merging with the Stoke Victoria Athletic Club in 1878, they took over their home, the Athletic Ground, and changed their name to Stoke. They moved to the Victoria Ground in 1883; it had a running track around the edge, one stand on the west side and banking around the other three sides. Before the turn of the century a pavilion was built next to the stand and in 1904 a cover was added to the banking opposite. In 1922 the original stand was replaced with a new main stand. Three years later Stoke FC changed its name to Stoke City FC. By 1930 the running track was dug up so the banking at the south end of the ground could be extended to cope with rising crowds. The covered banking on the east side of the pitch was replaced by a new 5,000-seater stand in 1936 at a time when the Potters boasted one of football's all-time greats, Stanley Matthews.

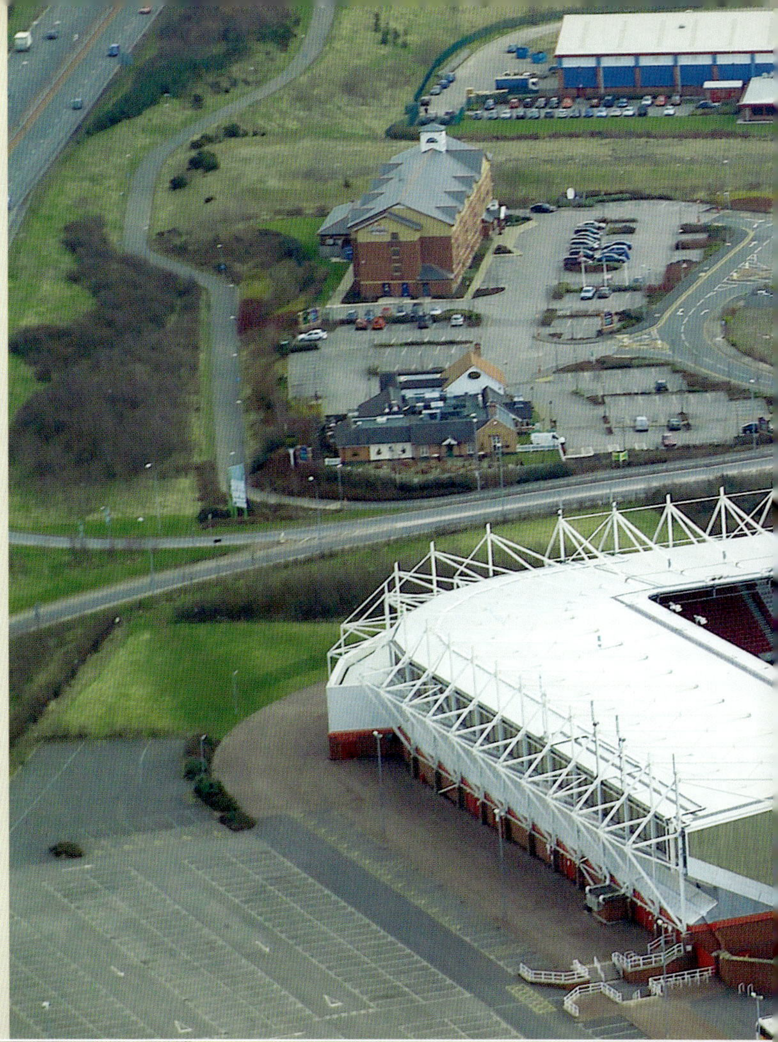

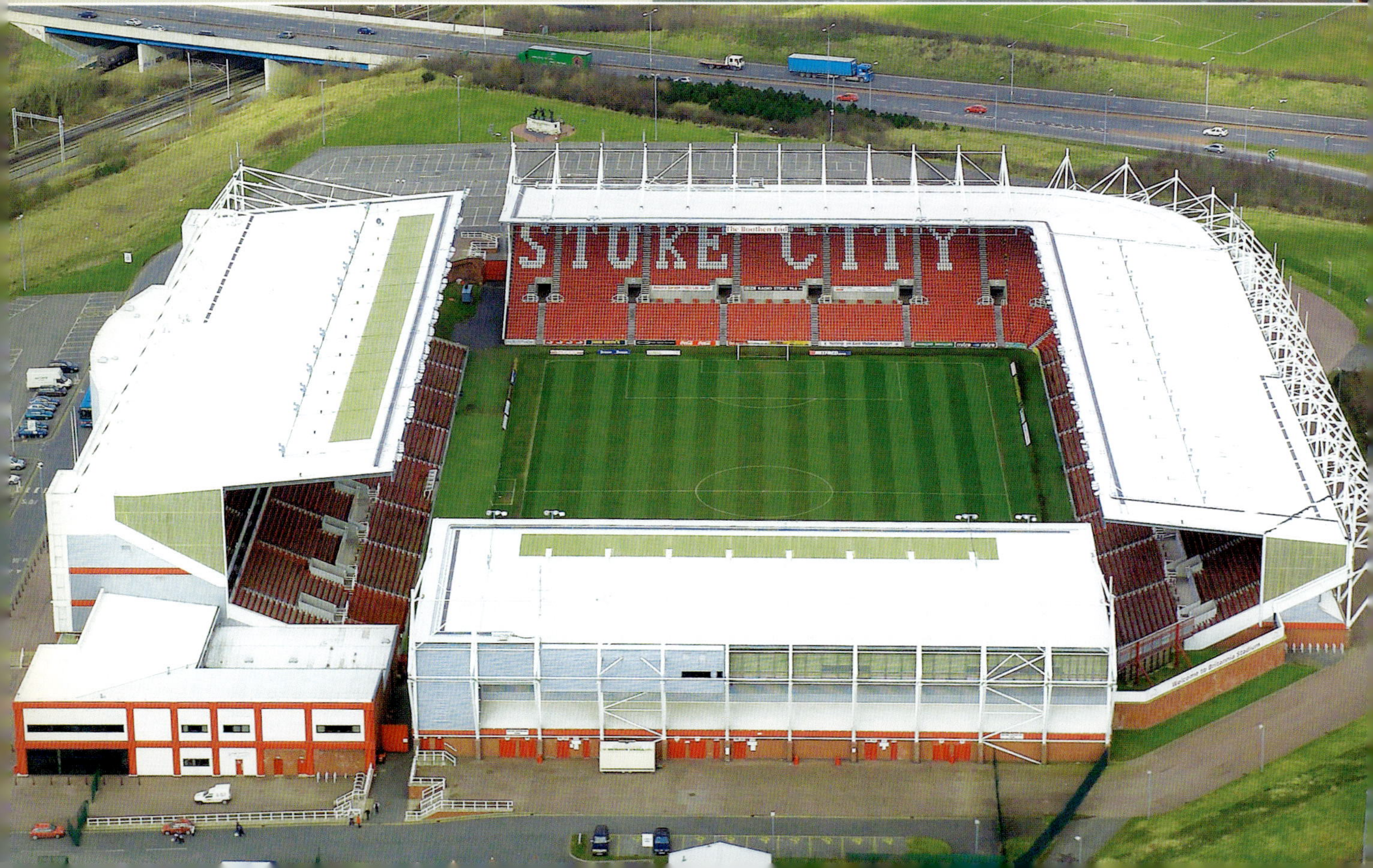

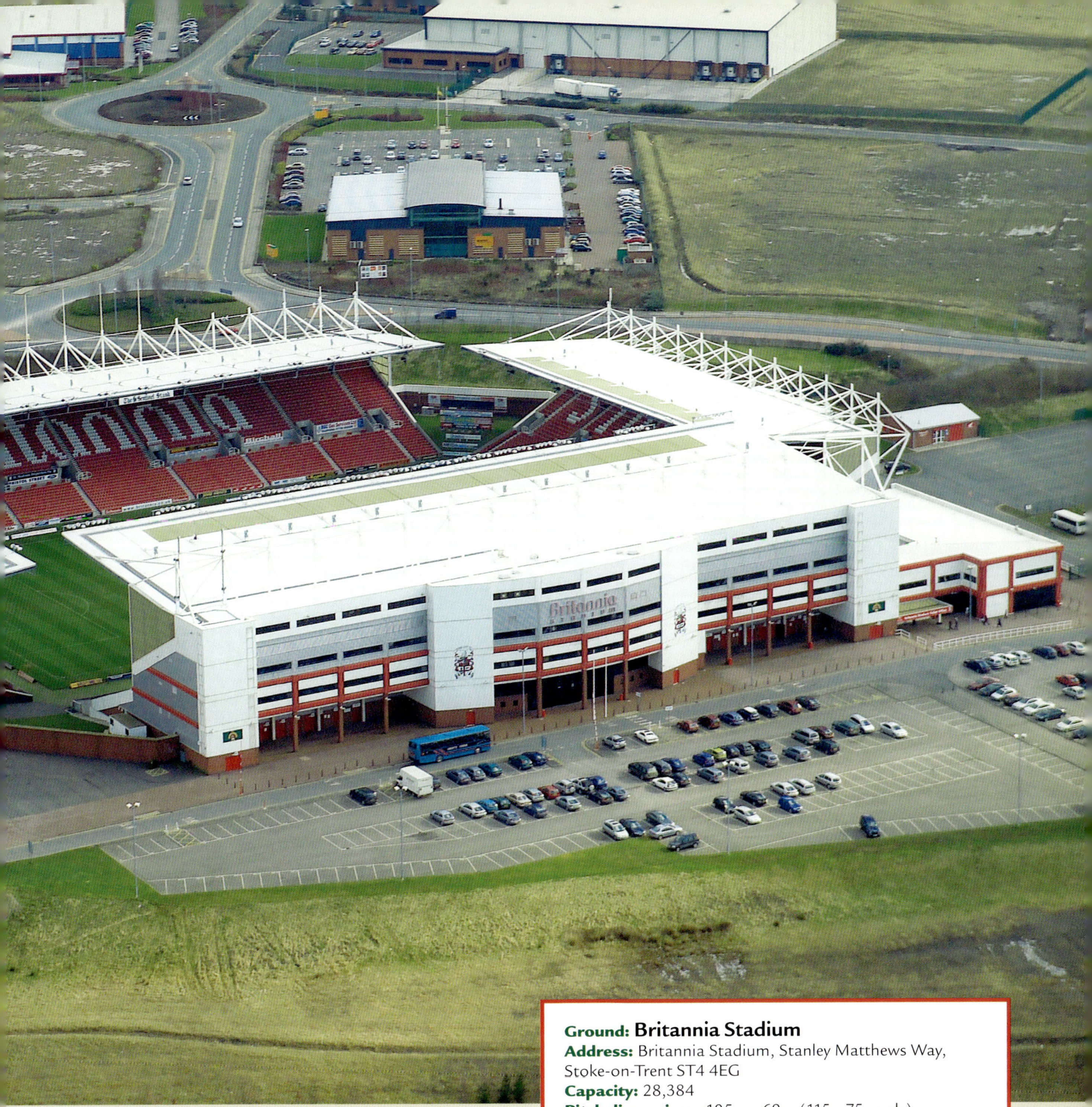

Ground: **Britannia Stadium**
Address: Britannia Stadium, Stanley Matthews Way, Stoke-on-Trent ST4 4EG
Capacity: 28,384
Pitch dimensions: 105m x 69m (115 x 75 yards)
Record attendance: (at the Victoria Ground) 51,380 vs Arsenal, March 29 1937

A year later the Victoria Ground saw its highest ever attendance of 51,380 for a game against Arsenal. The 1930s also saw the terraces concreted and the pitch shifted southwards. It was another 30 years before any further significant developments took place. In 1963 the Main Stand was replaced for the second time and the roof was replaced on the Butler Street Stand (East Stand) after a gale blew it off. A new two-tiered stand was built on the site of the north terrace in 1979. The Potters opted to sell the Victoria Ground in 1997 and moved to the Britannia Stadium, which was built on the site of a former colliery and ironworks. The new stadium has one stand curving round the north and east side and two separate stands on the south and west sides. It has a capacity of 28,384.

WEST BROMWICH ALBION

Ground: **The Hawthorns**
Address: Halfords Lane, West Bromwich, West Midlands B71 4LF
Capacity: 28,003
Pitch dimensions: 105m x 68m (115 x 74 yards)
Record attendance: 64,815 vs Arsenal, March 6 1937

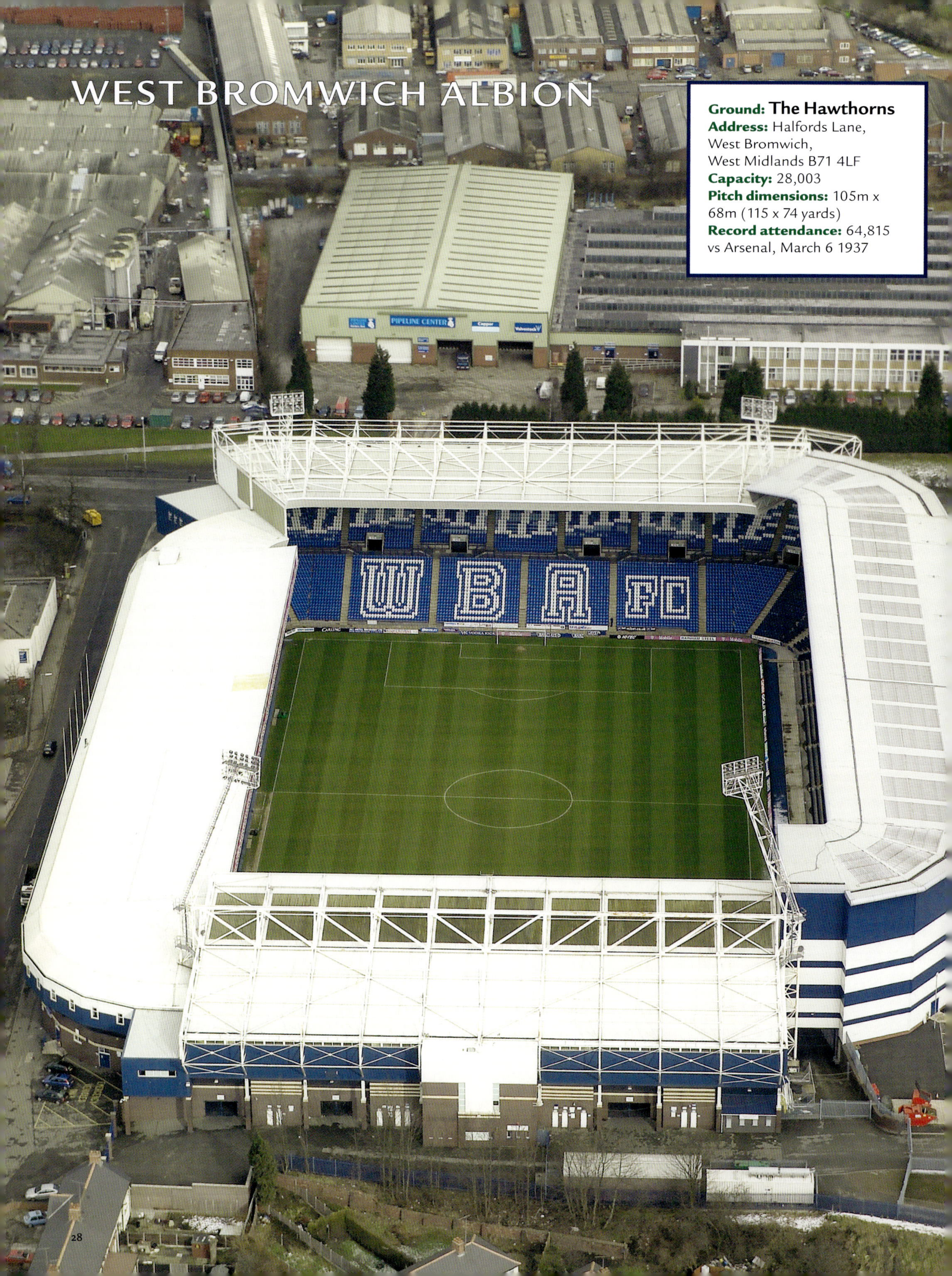

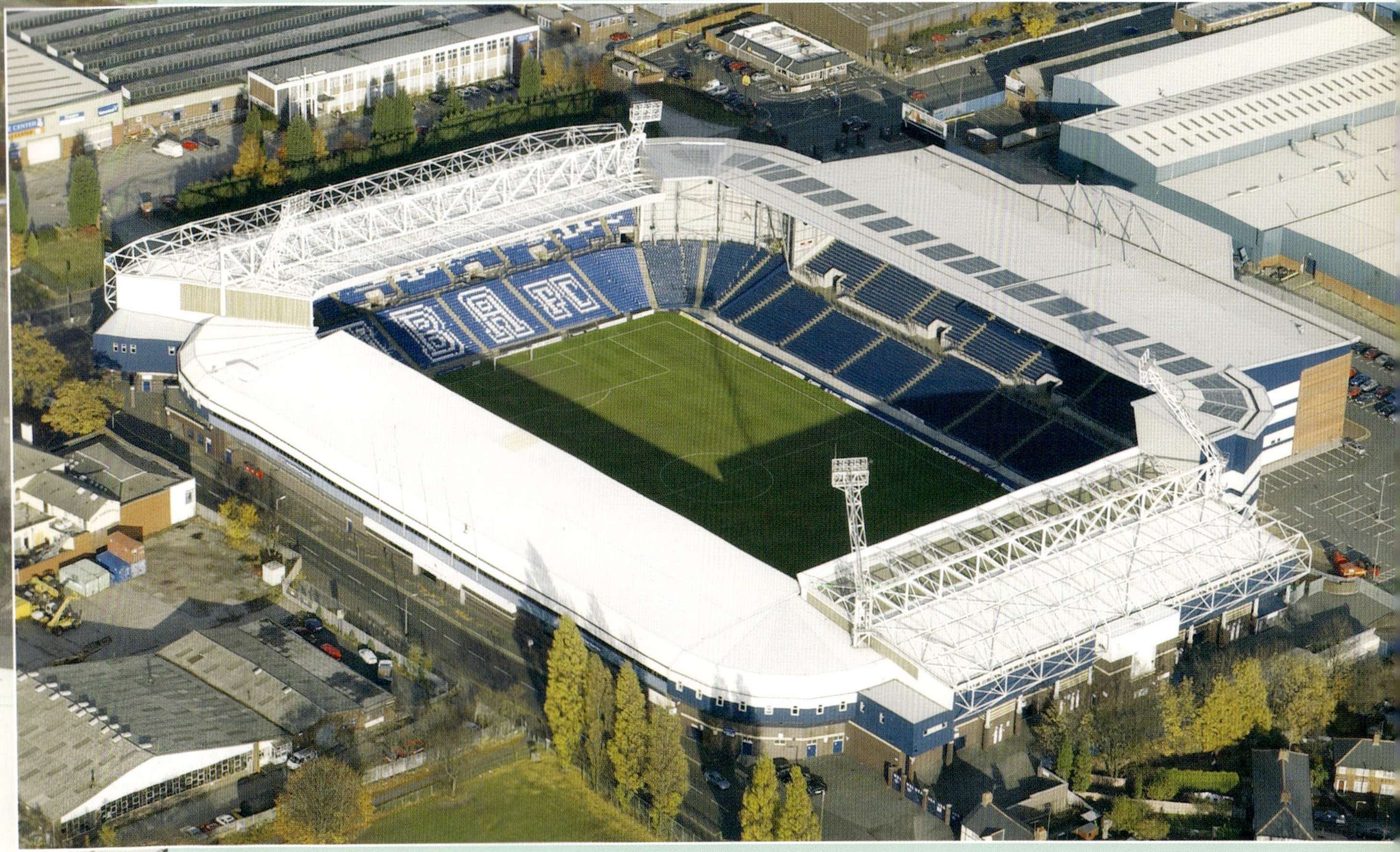

West Bromwich Albion FC was created by a group of workers from Salter's Spring Works in 1878. More than 100 years after they formed, they are one of only a few English football clubs to have won all three major honours – the League title, the FA Cup and the League Cup. They originally called themselves the West Bromwich Strollers after walking to nearby Wednesbury to buy themselves a ball. The name stuck until 1880, when they changed their name to the more familiar Albion. The club played at five different grounds before settling at The Hawthorns in 1900, a name that developed because the ground was once surrounded by hawthorn bushes. Situated between Birmingham and Sandwell, the initial capacity was 35,500 but when the club bought the ground's freehold in 1913 it began to develop the stands.

Concrete terracing was installed in 1920 and by 1924 the capacity reached 65,000. Terracing was completed on all four sides of the ground in 1931, the year the club won the FA Cup for the third time and gained promotion to the First Division.

In 1937 the ground saw a record attendance as 64,815 fans watched the Baggies take on Arsenal in the sixth round of the FA Cup. The more familiar stands of today were constructed between the 1940s and the 1960s. The East Stand, known as the Rainbow Stand because of its multi-coloured seats, was built on the site of the former Handsworth Stand. Improvements continued to the Birmingham Road End, which was covered in 1964, and the Halfords Lane side. The 1960s also saw the emergence of the Baggies' two most prolific scorers, Jeff Astle and Tony Brown. Following the Taylor report, a £4.15m all-seater stadium was opened in 1995. The Rainbow Stand was finally demolished in 2001 to make way for the new East Stand. When it opened in 2002 to a 1-0 defeat by Grimsby, The Hawthorns finally became fully enclosed.

WOLVERHAMPTON WANDERERS

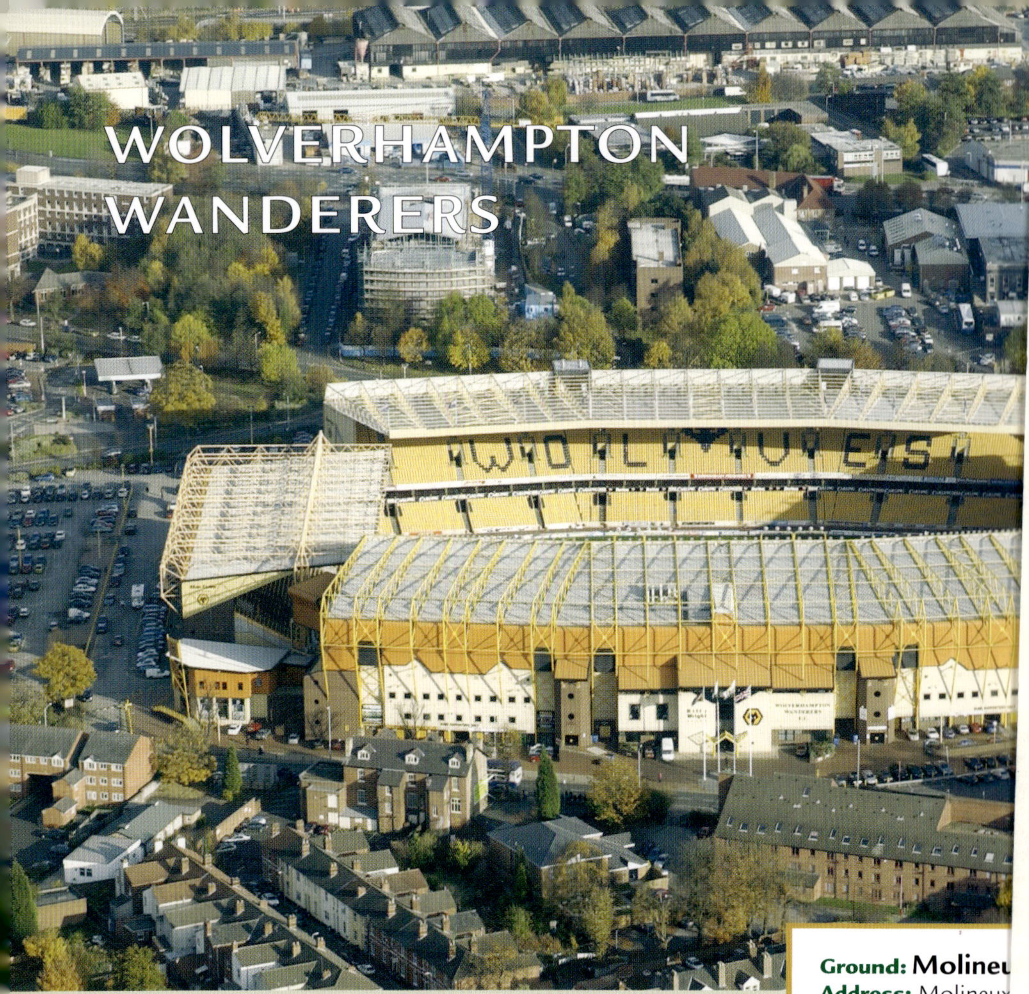

Ground: **Molineu**
Address: Molineux
Wolverhampton W
Capacity: 28,500
Pitch dimensions:
Record attendanc
February 11 1939

Wolves formed from a schoolboys team, St Lukes, in 1877, which then merged with a local cricket and football team, The Wanderers, in 1879 to form Wolverhampton Wanderers. After playing home games at Goldthorn Hill and Dudley Road, in 1889 the club moved to Molineux, a ground with a long history of hosting sporting events. A grandstand was built which could seat 300 spectators with shelter for a further 4,000 fans. Wolves played their first League game in 1889 against Notts County, which they won 2-0. Despite boasting a capacity of 20,000, it was not until 1925 that the major stands were built. The first was erected on the Waterloo Road side of the ground. The Molineux Street Stand was rebuilt in 1932 after a gale blew the old cover down. This distinctive structure had a multi-span roof, with a clock mounted in the centre. The 1930s saw the north and south end terracing covered to shelter the large crowds that flocked to home games. During this period, 61,315 fans turned up to see Wolves take on Liverpool, the largest crowd ever recorded at the ground. During the 1950s, Molineux was best known for its newly installed floodlights. Top European clubs flocked to the Midlands ground to enjoy

the opportunities o
possible by this nov
led to the demolitic
in its place a £2m g
almost led to the cl
with the debt but i
council, who bougl
Sir Jack Hayward p
estimated £20m, r
most modern in th
up of four separat
Stand, was openec
sat on top of the o
1930s was incorpo
other stands were
Harris Stand, comp
ground are two famous statues – one of Billy Wright and the other of former player and manager Stan Cullis.

GBU
Association des Gro
Universitaires de Fra
21, rue Serpente
75006 Paris
www.gbu.fr

DANS LA MÊME COLLECTION
L'évangile : un message honteux
Si Dieu existe, pourquoi le mal ?
Sexe et désir : fruits défendus ou *de Jonathan Hanley*
Le désespoir, quelle issue ? *de W*
Médias : quelle (télé) vision ? *de I et Alain Stamp*
La Trinité : mystère futile ou réal
Vivre dans un monde créé, *de Ly*

B.P. 20
77421 Marne-la-V
1re édition : décembre 2007
Les références bibliques ont été tradu originaux (hébreux et grecs).
Couverture : Jacques Maré – IOTA
Composition : Éditions Farel
Impression : IMÉAF, 26160 La Bégud
Dépôt légal : décembre 2007 — N° d'i
ISBN : 978-2-86314-363-6
ISNN : 1774-3311

Introduction

Dieu est-il cohérent ? Question à la limite de l'impertinence ou de l'inconscience : comment un être humain, si tâtonnant et balbutiant pour essayer d'élaborer une *pensée* cohérente et plus encore pour conduire une *action* cohérente, pourrait-il décemment entrer en débat avec Dieu sur ce sujet ? Faudra-t-il, à peine la question posée, la déclarer irrecevable et clore prématurément ce livre au titre sacrilège ?

Non, car Dieu, si l'on en croit la Bible, ne semble pas, quant à lui, exclure un tel questionnement, si audacieux soit-il. N'est-ce pas sur la cohérence de l'action divine qu'Abraham s'interroge lorsqu'il pose cette question osée : « Le juge de toute la terre n'agirait-il pas selon l'équité ? » (Genèse 18.25). Le dialogue, Dieu le souhaite et l'entretient, parce qu'il comprend que l'être humain puisse ne pas saisir d'emblée la cohérence de son action. Le dialogue, il le souhaite même au point de faire de l'être humain un réel partenaire de son action. C'est bien ainsi qu'il considère Abraham lorsqu'il lui fait part de son intention de détruire Sodome : « Cacherais-je à Abraham ce que je vais faire ? » (Genèse 18.18).

Osons donc la question tout en nous souvenant que c'est d'abord nous qui risquons de ne pas comprendre ou de mal comprendre la cohérence de la pensée et de l'action de Dieu.

Cette pensée et cette action de Dieu, la Bible nous les donne à comprendre en deux étapes bien marquées que l'on appelle ancienne et nouvelle alliances et qui correspondent aux deux parties de la Bible, l'Ancien et le Nouveau Testament [1]. C'est à ce

1 Alliance et testament sont en fait deux manières différentes et approximatives pour rendre en français le même mot qui, dans la langue originale, hébreu ou grec, désigne les dispositions prises par Dieu pour

propos que la question de la cohérence de Dieu se trouve souvent posée : on oppose l'image de Dieu inquiétante, voire terrifiante qu'imposerait l'Ancien Testament à l'image plus rassurante du Nouveau. Cette opposition trouve au moins une part de justification dans la phrase bien connue qui forme la conclusion du prologue de l'Évangile selon Jean : « La loi a été donnée par Moïse, la grâce et la vérité sont venues par Jésus-Christ. » (Jean 1.17). La différence, incontestable, entre les deux alliances est signalée et soulignée par le double contraste : celui des *figures* emblématiques, Moïse et Jésus-Christ, et celui des *thèmes* ou principes, la loi d'un côté, la grâce et la vérité de l'autre.

Cette différence n'empêche pas pour autant que, d'une alliance à l'autre, le même Dieu poursuive le même dessein dont les deux alliances sont les deux étapes distinctes et coordonnées. Les auteurs du Nouveau Testament en sont profondément persuadés ; ils en donnent constamment la preuve.

Tout au long de l'histoire de l'Église, les chrétiens, notamment les théologiens, n'ont cessé de s'interroger sur l'articulation entre les deux alliances et d'élaborer des modèles conceptuels pour en rendre compte. D'autres ouvrages s'emploient à exposer et à comparer ces modèles. La voie que l'on entend suivre ici pour percevoir la cohérence du dessein de Dieu est celle de l'étude biblique, de la théologie biblique. On propose de saisir quatre thèmes majeurs d'un livre de l'Ancien Testament, le livre de l'Exode, en s'efforçant de comprendre, pour chacun d'eux, la cohérence de l'action de Dieu d'une alliance à l'autre.

Chacun de ces thèmes correspond à une partie importante de l'ouvrage. Le premier, *Dieu libère,* coïncide avec la première moitié du livre (chapitres 1-15), le second, *Dieu donne sa loi,* avec la seconde moitié (chapitres 19-40). Le troisième, *Dieu pardonne,* on le rattachera à l'épisode du veau d'or (chapitres 32-34). Contrairement aux deux précédents, le récit n'occupe que trois chapitres du livre, mais il rapporte un événement majeur dont la thématique ne peut se réduire à celle de la libération ou du don de la loi. C'est à la faveur de ce même récit que l'on abordera le sujet de la *présence de Dieu*, qui, lui aussi, sous-tend l'ensemble du livre. À l'énoncé des quatre thèmes, on aura compris que l'on touche au cœur de la révélation biblique.

---

garantir à ses partenaires humains des relations définies et stables : Dieu s'y engage et précise ce qu'il attend de l'être humain.

CHAPITRE 1

Dieu libère (Exode 1-15)

Dieu libère : thème majeur de tout l'Ancien Testament. Dieu a choisi de se faire connaître dans l'histoire comme celui qui a libéré le peuple d'Israël de l'esclavage en Égypte. On le comprend. L'image est éminemment positive : Dieu en défenseur des opprimés, des parias, Dieu prenant le parti des faibles contre la plus grande puissance de l'époque et parvenant à les libérer. Manifestation de sa puissance et de sa justice.

En désignant de manière systématique le peuple opprimé comme les *Hébreux*, terme utilisé de manière hostile et méprisante par les Égyptiens, le récit souligne à quel point Dieu fait cause commune avec les opprimés. C'est d'abord comme porte-parole du *Dieu des Hébreux* que Moïse devait se présenter devant le pharaon : « Yahvé, le Dieu des Hébreux, nous est apparu. Permets-nous de faire trois journées de marche dans le désert pour offrir des sacrifices à Yahvé, notre Dieu. » (Exode 3.18). Moïse, le moment venu, prenant quelque liberté avec les consignes reçues, s'adressera au pharaon de manière impériale, au nom de Yahvé, le Dieu d'*Israël* : « Ainsi parle Yahvé, le Dieu d'Israël : laisse aller mon peuple pour qu'il célèbre une fête en mon honneur. » (Exode 5.1). Après la réponse cinglante du pharaon : « Qui est Yahvé pour que j'obéisse à sa voix ? » (Exode 5.2), Moïse se voit contraint de reformuler sa demande de manière nettement plus modeste : « Le Dieu des Hébreux nous est apparu. Permets-nous de faire trois journées de marche dans le désert … » (Exode 5.3).

Le récit fait ressortir le caractère odieux de la puissance asservissante. On y retrouve les traits des régimes oppressifs qui ont sévi et ne cessent de sévir tout au long de l'histoire. L'argumentaire xénophobe, qui exagère la menace : « Voici le peuple des Israélites est devenu plus nombreux et plus fort que nous. » (1.9) [1]. Les travaux forcés, utilisés non seulement pour réaliser une économie de main-d'œuvre, mais aussi pour décimer les populations qui y sont astreintes. L'emploi d'auxiliaires parmi les Hébreux pour diviser le peuple. Jusqu'aux mesures d'élimination directe à la naissance : « Jetez dans le fleuve tout garçon qui naîtra et laissez vivre toutes les filles. » (1.22).

D'autres traits apparaissent encore : le refus de tout congé, même pour motif religieux [2], la surenchère dans la cruauté qui consiste à répondre à des demandes d'allègement par un renforcement des contraintes [3], le jeu du chat et de la souris où l'on promet pour revenir au dernier moment sur ce qui avait été promis, enfin l'acharnement extrême, qui amène le pharaon à poursuivre encore les Hébreux, même après les avoir chassés [4].

On comprend que cette image si positive du Dieu qui libère ait

---

1 À partir de maintenant, toutes les citations tirées du livre de l'Exode ne mentionneront que chapitres et versets. Seules les citations d'autres livres de la Bible mentionneront le titre du livre.

2 Réponse du pharaon : « Ce sont des paresseux ; voilà pourquoi ils crient : Allons offrir des sacrifices à notre Dieu ! » (5.8).

3 « Vous ne donnerez plus, comme d'habitude, de la paille au peuple pour faire des briques ; qu'ils aillent eux-mêmes s'en ramasser. Vous leur imposerez néanmoins la quantité de briques qu'ils faisaient d'habitude, vous ne la diminuerez en rien. » (5.7-8).

4 « Les sentiments du pharaon et des gens de sa cour changèrent à l'égard du peuple. Ils dirent : Qu'avons-nous fait en laissant partir Israël, alors qu'il était à notre service ? Le pharaon attela son char et prit son peuple avec lui. » (14.5-6).